PRAGUE SYMPHONY

A.M.D.G.,

Mark

Prague Symphony

A Requiem for the Cold War

MARK ALLEN

PRAHA PUBLISHING

ISBN: 978-0-9818067-1-6

CONTENTS

Dedicated to the soul of Virgil Victor Brallier, 1915-2006
"My peace, not as the world gives, I give to you."

They say the best men are moulded out of faults,
And, for the most, become much more the better
for being a little bad.

William Shakespeare

Suppose then, that we are wanderers in a strange country, and could not live happily away from our fatherland, and that we felt wretched in our wandering, and wishing to put an end to our misery, determined to return home. We find, however, that we must make use of some mode of conveyance, either by land or by water, in order to reach that fatherland where our enjoyment is to commence. But the beauty of the country through which we pass, and the very pleasure of the motion, charm our hearts, and turning these things which we ought to use into objects of enjoyment, we became unwilling to hasten the end of our journey; and becoming engrossed in a factitious delight, our thoughts are diverted from that home whose delights would make us truly happy.

Augustine of Hippo

PREFACE

THIS book took me nearly twenty years to write – during only eighteen months of which did I actually put down a single word. And it covers, excepting just a few detours and introductions, only *twenty-four* months: those immediately following the collapse of Communism in Europe. You will soon see those months through the eyes of a young American man trying to find his place and his way in that changing yet changeless world.

Those two years had an intense impact on me. *So* intense in fact that I spent a decade-and-a-half, for reasons I still don't fully understand, trying to wash them out of my system. Trying to forget their voices, their lessons, and their promises.

Almost immediately upon my return to the States in 1992, I tried to invent a simpler new me. I tried to live humbly and anonymously as an ordinary American and to mask the fact that I am, essentially, an intellectual and an aesthete. And that I am plagued (or blessed?) with quintessentially European spiritual hungers. I sought to lose myself in nature and in numbers, and to ignore the more dangerous world of ideas. To block out all reminders of understandings beyond the mundane, and to be someone other than myself.

But when my grandfather died, all the rich music that I lived with in central Europe came back to me, and I had to sit down and write. I had to be me.

The Communist regime in Czechoslovakia was overthrown peacefully in the final weeks of 1989 by a massive spiritual revival whose credo was simply this: "Truth and Love will triumph over

Lies and Hate." Millions of people actually believed that. And as incredible as *that* sounds, they went even further — they proved this belief to be true.

I liked the melodramatic schmarm of those words so much that I almost entitled this book "Love, Hate, Truth, and Lies" — despite that title's unforgivable sexlessness. I confess that aesthetic lapse to you now in order to confess further that you *will* find all four of those elements in this book. It is the fourth element that I must especially draw your attention to, since some of the *Lies* contained in this book are my own. Of those, they are a mixed bunch: Most are unintentional, since my memory is faulty and my education incomplete. A few others are harmless rearrangements of personal episodes that I have made consciously for practical or personal reasons.

Less harmless perhaps is the fact that my personal perceptions and prejudices have, without question, colored this work. And done so in ways that some readers, with *different* perceptions and different prejudices, will find troubling. I just ask your mercy. I have tried to be intensely honest in this book, and I ask you to be forgiving if, *in your eyes*, I do not attain perfection in that regard.

My goal in writing this story has been to "*see into the life of things,*" not to create a dry dispatch that could stand the scrutiny of a meticulous fact checker and come back unmarked. If I have failed to convey valuable and lasting truths, only *then* I will feel like I have failed. And only you can be the judge of that.

Since I've already mentioned my grandfather, to whom this book is dedicated, one thing must be dispensed with here: Who is the author of this book? Well, me. But who is "me"? Well, that depends. If you look on the cover, you will see clearly that this book was written by "Mark Allen" – me. But if you look *under* the cover, and read this story, you will find reference to a paternal line of "Bralliers"; and one "Mark Brallier" will seem to be speaking in the first person.

Yes, a birth certificate printed on an Army base in New Jersey during the Vietnam War does in fact define the essence that is me as "Mark Allen Brallier." But in 1992, shortly after my tragicomic return from Czechoslovakia, I opted to become known more plainly as "Mark Allen." There is one simple and relatively innocent explanation for that strange falling off, which is this: I had become an entrepreneur and preferred not to start every sales call with a pronunciation lesson. And that's true. But there's perhaps a deeper side to this nominal transformation, and to get a sense of that you'll need to read the book.

There are of course (and thankfully) many other people besides me in this story, and I have changed a few of *their* names as well. I ask you please not to disturb the anonymous peace of those individuals whom I have thus attempted to protect. Thank you.

You will find within these pages, sticking out like random weeds, a handful of poems. These were all written in Czechoslovakia during the years this book covers, and pulled out of my journal. I have stuck them in this book primarily for my own benefit, since that is the only way I could ever manage to get them published and preserved. Thank you for your indulgence.

Besides poems, there are many other journal entries from these years that make their way into this work. Some of these are my own thoughts and, though written almost two decades ago by an immature young man, I have included them here because I think they help to convey the story I am trying to tell. And perhaps also because the adolescent who wrote them still has a vain desire to see them published. *Sic transit Gloria mundi.*

Many other journal entries from those years are not my thoughts at all, but simply the thoughts of others that I read at that time and that I felt worthy of copying down. I have included some of those too since they say what I'd like to say better than I ever could myself.

Much of what you are about to read is very personal. But I hope that you will find in this story much more than the inner workings of an idiosyncratic individual. I hope you will gain a deeper sense of history and of place. I hope you'll learn to have a greater appreciation for the unique character and culture of the Czech nation — and perhaps of your own. Most importantly, I hope you will re-remember, as I often must, that there's much more to heaven and earth than is dreamt of in your political philosophy. Perhaps this little book can serve as a reminder to us both.

Hopkinton, NH, USA
January 25, 2008

I. Largo affettuoso

I'M sure that eighteen years of democracy have blown them away by now, but when I lived in Czechoslovakia the ghosts of World War Two still loitered there grimly. They whispered softly in the winds, *"I'm still here … can't you hear me?"*

It's hard for me to say exactly what I mean by that, or why I say that, but I'm sure that any sensitive student of history who visited that country's quiet corners in 1990 heard those same sorrowful voices. They spoke of suffering and of might-have-beens not bitterly, but with a nostalgic and almost beautiful sadness.

These restless spirits could be heard best in small villages and country lanes, and I heard them clearer than ever one dark December morning as I stood on a dirt road beside a hayfield in a remote corner of northwestern Moravia. The wind blew cold through the evergreens, and a thick layer of clouds from one horizon to the other diffused the mid-morning sun so well that you could forget it was up there. The darkness, the permanence, the inevitability of history hung heavy in the winter air.

I have often struggled with the concept of collective guilt, and that day one voice in the distance had a special message for me. It intoned so quietly I could barely make it out over the whistling wind: *"Yalta …. Yalta … Yalta … "* The place where the fate of this beautiful and noble nation was once again to be determined by others; and where my president told Stalin, in 1945, that this little one could be his.

I mumbled back toward the trees, "I'm so … sorry." But words are meaningless in historical winds like these. *Es müss sein.*

As I stood there being buffeted by history, my surroundings suddenly transformed: Large snowflakes began dancing individually to the ground. First, in numbers small enough that each one caught my attention and seemed special. But gradually, imperceptibly, the snow started to come down in such quantity that it took great concentration to follow a single flake. Eventually one just had to give up and accept that is was really snowing, and that each individual flake did not really matter — it was simply something huge and beautiful of which one was blessed to be a part.

This was the same snow that covered the scattered steaming remains of a sixteen-year-old boy who had just been blown to pieces by a Soviet shell. And it covered the sturdy Mauser rifle he had been holding – which took the hit much better than the *jugend*'s soft, human flesh.

This was the same snow that fell on Mahler's disheveled hair when he lived here, bringing some peace to his troubled soul as its flakes turned to water in the heat of that singular brain.

This was the same snow that covered the field of a nearby collective farm: a field which six generations of God-fearing peasants had called their own until a red sickle harvested it out from under them. This land had known these men by name, and it missed their calloused hands and knees, which used to pray on its dusty soil for rain or a beautiful wife.

This snow has covered lots of other painful things that nobody, except perhaps for the gracious God that sent it, remembers now. It fell softly on me saying, *"Let it go Mark. It's OK."*

I did not forget those words, but I did not really listen to them until my grandfather died.

Though he bore the name of a pagan poet, my grandfather was in fact a clergyman and a Communist. Yes, a man of faith.

Virgil came from a long line of passionate iconoclasts, so perhaps such beliefs shouldn't be surprising. His great-great-great-grandfather took a heretical faith so seriously that he decided, in 1769, to uproot wife and children from the richest garden in the world. Christian wanted his family to worship God purely, far from the corruption of Catholic king and pope, in the English New World.

That proud Huguenot died beside his wife within hours of seeing paradise; and then may or may not have seen Paradise. But regardless of this eternal unanswerable, we do know that his three sons survived for a while to continue, on a new continent, Christian's odd legacy.

The orphans were bound out to German farmers in western Pennsylvania to work the rocky soil six days per week. On the seventh they rested on rough-hewn pews and had their wicked young minds cleansed in the clear waters of Baptist theology.

One of these boys had been a confused pubescent Frenchman of twelve when his father freed him of Catholic tyranny and dragged him off to freedom God-knows-where. A dozen years later Emmanuel found himself called an "American," and found himself holding a smoking musket at a place called Yorktown. Things were not going well for his regiment when Emmanuel cried out (in English of course) "I hope the French will help soon or all is lost!" As if on cue, French soldiers serving under a Catholic king came, quite accidentally, to the aid of this Protestant traitor bred in that same far-away garden.

Thanks to those Frenchmen, Emmanuel *did* survive the battle of Yorktown, and lived to breed in his adopted homeland. And so now my daughters have the right to possess a document proclaiming them aristocrats in this fine democratic land of ours. They can proudly prove that at least one of their ancestors fought in the war that rid this land of hereditary honors — and all the destructive vanity that they engender.

A mere century after Emmanuel died of old age, far from the bloody battlefield, his great-great-grandson Virgil learned to read the family Bible on a dusty mid-western farm.

Though he would later lose the traditional faith of Christian, in his own way Grandpa never lost connection with his past. Because for him, that past was defined by poverty. No otherworldly nonsense could talk the poor out of him. He was born poor, raised poor, and carefully remained poor for all of his 91 years — it was that important to him.

I don't know exactly when Virgil met Lenin on the road to Damascus, but I'd guess it was sometime in the 50's while he was working toward his PhD in Boston. In those days many thousands of Americans intelligent enough to earn a PhD were *also* intelligent enough to appreciate Stalin's blessings — I don't think my grandfather was unusually perceptive in this regard.

But I do think he must have been a misfit in this new Leftist circle of his. Not only because he wore the hated cloth, but even more because he was a humble kid from the flatlands and he smiled a lot. Most of his comrades were boastful Brookline WASP's or bitter Brooklyn Jews. And they didn't smile all that much.

In the 1960's, when I was born, Grandpa lived with his adoring wife and their five eclectic offspring in an idyllic parsonage set in the rolling hills of Western Massachusetts. His nearest neighbor, and intellectual confidant, was a Jewish playboy from Manhattan who escaped the complicated webs he wove in The City by driving up to the Berkshires and hiding in a dark fieldstone cottage.

The most vivid memories of my childhood are of that sunny parsonage, that shady cottage, and the lush hayfields nearby. The parsonage stood on its own beside a huge rolling field; I see it now with Andrew Wyeth's eyes. Mr. Stein's stone house stayed far out of the sun — hiding in a dense stand of ancient trees. That place's chilly darkness was foreboding to me, and I observed it only from the safety of my grandparents' warm and sunny driveway. Near the distant base of that drive, and running perpendicular to it, a neat row of fat sugar maples towered majestically to tell me where my safe world ended and the mysterious outside world began.

In this rich setting I was simultaneously introduced to the world of nature and the world of ideas. At the time, I felt no disconnect between the two: it was just life, in all its mystery and majesty.

While crunching on rhubarb stalk out in his garden, Grandpa

would often share his thoughts with me, and ask me questions I couldn't fully understand.

Though he was a professional preacher, I never once heard him mention "Jesus" or "sin" or "salvation." He seemed to prefer sharing his "new ways of thinking about things."

A name Grandpa *did* invoke now and then was "God". But when he did so I could tell by the way he tilted his head and raised the pitch of his voice that he was talking about something or someone very different from the omnipotent and jealous *"I am"* whom Abraham knew and loved and feared.

One day, when I was about seven, I overheard my grandmother complain about a troublesome parishioner who was going around fomenting mutiny by telling the sheepish townsfolk that my grandfather "wasn't preaching the Gospel of Christ." I remember understanding intuitively that this nameless enemy was onto something dangerous and powerful. That he needed to be silenced.

On another memorable occasion about that same year, I sat at the kitchen table in the parsonage and daydreamed while adults spoke just a bit over my not-entirely-innocent head. I followed their lead and dreamed about how wonderful the world could be if individuals did not have so much freedom, and if a central authority directed their actions toward the common good. And I understood very well how important it was to make sure that the *whole world* followed this same authority: because if just one island of independent selfishness remained the whole beautiful scheme would be thrown out of whack.

These sorts of heaven-on-earth dreams informed my mind and soul even beyond the point when testosterone first confused me with *new* dreams.

And then, at age sixteen, I watched my best friend die in a tangled mess of metal, blood, and broken glass. His death rattle shook for only a minute, but I lay pinned beside his pale silent corpse for two long hours with my own toes poking me in the stomach.

I stared endlessly at my confidant's motionless essence in

complete confusion. I kept wondering over and over, *"What's wrong with Mike? What's ... wrong ... with ... Mike? What?!!"* I knew that something very significant had changed about him. But no matter how many times I asked myself that simple question, I couldn't come up with any sort of answer.

The next day, while seated beside my hospital bed, my father gave it to me in exquisitely simple terms: "Mark, Mike died."

Tears welled as I choked on the words, "Yeah, I knew that." I could finally cry now – now that someone had given my friend's mysterious transformation a name.

That same year my grandfather's utopian dreams lost their power to inspire me. And sadly, the preacher had planted nothing else in me to take their place.

Into a vacuum of nothingness, my soul tumbled. And I fell asleep.

Four years later I somehow found myself reading *The Closing of the American Mind* and it woke me from the dead. It blasted bright light into the dark corners of my soul when it stated, with the authority of three thousand years, that some things are inherently true and others are inherently false; some beautiful, some ugly; some good, some bad; some noble, some ignoble. And for some strange reason I could not even begin to comprehend, these radical concepts inspired me and gave me hope.

Though the author did not say so, I began to infer from his strange words that there must be an eternal power behind these ancient new truths. And I began to resent my grandfather: I blamed him for my spiritual malaise.

My adolescent bitterness found its desired focus one afternoon when I was thumbing through Grandpa's extensive library and found a book with this handwritten inscription under the cover:

For Virgil, with fond memories of our cell meeting.[*]

May 1, 1955

"You hypocritical *bastard!*"

My newfound love of books and learning coupled itself that day with an intense hatred of Communism and all utopian isms. I resolved to enter to fight on the other side, and to undo some of the damage my grandfather and his friends had wrought on me and souls like mine.

---

* i.e. a Communist Party cell meeting.

WHAT

What is a road rarely real
leading to why
And how.

DIVERTIMENTO: *MIT HUMOR*

I made plans that year to go to law school, but don't exactly know why. I guess I felt it would teach me to flex my growing brain muscle more effectively, and make me a more effective soldier in the crusade for which I had just signed myself up.

When I finally finished my honors thesis and graduated college, in December 1989, I moved from Connecticut to Arlington, VA. I didn't have a car, but I could walk to the metro and be in downtown D.C. very easily. I spent most of my free time attending free chamber music concerts at the Library of Congress, sightseeing, and just wandering around the marble city. A few times I was invited, through my new job, to attend a function on Capitol Hill where I mingled with Senators, Congressmen, and other vermin.

It was an interesting scene to say the least. Alcohol, surprisingly, was a big part of it. Not for me, I mean for the politicians and their hangers-on.

More than a few of the right-wingers I met were Southern Baptists … a breed I don't think I had ever met before. Word around town was that these guys didn't drink at all, but I remember one in particular sipping on a Coors beer and speaking in irritated tones about how "everybody around here seems to think they know what being a Southern Baptist means." Personally, I had *no idea* what it meant … but I guess I was learning.

My work was pretty dull, but it did allow me a three-month window into a world I thought would be mine. I quickly realized that I didn't fit in there, and felt almost nauseous at times. That's exaggerating, but only a little. The power was palpable and intoxicating, but it had a very dark side that was never far from the surface. At least that's how it seemed to me.

As for the job, I was a lowly intern working temporarily as the "Recruitment Director" for a right-wing political organization based in the distant suburbs. Basically what I did was spend all day on the phone calling the leaders of various conservative organizations all over the country and asking them "so how may people are you bringing with you to the class next week?" Not exactly the intellectual glory I had in mind when I first entered this crusade.

The Arlington "intern house" I lived in belonged to this organization, and I shared it with about five other young guys with political ambitions. We lived right across the river from downtown D.C., which was pretty convenient. Since we worked out in the burbs, all of us would commute together by car against the traffic. While everyone else was heading *toward* the city, we were heading away … and visa versa. This worked well, though I would have preferred to take the Metro into town — as I did most weekends and many evenings.

Living with us also were two "house parents" — an illiterate 40-something couple from Louisiana who'd been given free housing (with indoor plumbing!) in exchange for keeping an eye on the boys and make sure nothing got out of hand – i.e. that no girls ever stepped foot inside. These unworldly bumpkins were old acquaintances of Morton Blackwell, the founder of the organization, and they were the butt of everyone's jokes … except Morton's of course. Morton didn't like anyone slandering anybody, let alone his loyal cronies.

Of my roommates, I only remember one of those guys very well – Tony Storch. Tony was from Florida, and had driven a tank in the Marines. That was his past life, but when I knew him he looked more like a Grateful Deadhead. He usually wore tie-dyed t-shirts and colorful wool caps — which suited his easy-going appearance well but which contrasted strangely with his passion for military history and his encyclopedic knowledge on that subject. The art and science of war is a serious subject if there ever was one, but Tony nonetheless always remained jovial and happy … a roly-poly Falstaff who happened also to be a scholar of death.

Tony was by far the most animated of our bunch, and I recall vividly the night we all watched Buster Douglas knock out Mike

Tyson, beating 50/1 odds. Tony jumped up in the air, doubled over in disbelief, and shouted joyous obscenities for five minutes straight. He was always a man of extreme (and seemingly sincere) exclamations.

I ran into Tony again — purely by chance — almost a year later at a party for Americans in Czechoslovakia. Tony was classic Tony. To show his amazement at the odds of this chance encounter he sprayed a mouthful of beer all over the table, just barely missing the pretty blonde from Alabama beside him.

While he wiped his mouth and tried to compose himself well enough to speak, the Alabama girl smiled, touched my arm, and said to me kindly in her soft drawl, "I see there's some emotion here!" With a quick subtle glance I surmised that this *belle* was just a little too plump for my tastes as I replied, "Yeah, I guess so."

Sorry, I'm getting ahead of myself: back to D.C. My employers traveled all over the country, training right-wingers in the logistics of winning elections. I only traveled with them once, and I can't even remember where it was. Denver maybe? No, Milwaukee I think. We never left the airport hotel so it didn't matter anyway. I was actually in the class just like any other student. I guess they wanted me to experience what I was selling over the phone every day.

All I remember about that class is spending literally twenty hours per day, for three days straight, in a hotel conference room. We moved around from one circular table to another talking strategy and making plans for an imaginary election. From an insider, I later learned that the sleep deprivation was very intentional and an important part of the training – they wanted to see how you worked under stress.

While everyone was hashing out make-believe election issues with strangers, a couple of experienced operatives sat in the distance on opposite sides of the room and took notes. These two never looked up once from their notepads, and successfully avoided eye contact with anyone. I learned later from that same insider that their notes on me were not flattering at all — I did not pass this trial by fire.

But that didn't seem to bother Morton at all; he wanted to groom me for office. It seems he thought I had "what it takes to win elections." Not as an operative, but as a candidate. This pissed off my boss to no end.

Kevin Gentry was his name, and he was an obnoxious Richmond, Virginia boy who enjoyed referring to the Civil War as "The War of Northern Aggression," and refused to say anything at all about the founder of his party.

Kevin was just a little shorter than me, with very pale skin, short black hair, and a funny jerky walk. He smiled much too much, crooked his head sideways, and shook hands in such a way that you wanted to wash up quickly lest his evil soul permeate your skin. I despised him, and the feeling was mutual even before *his* boss took a shine to me.

But there were other right-wingers I worked with that I really liked. One was Charlie Arlinghaus. He came from the Detroit suburbs and was very smart and articulate. He had a funny nasal way of talking that got your attention quickly, and then his words kept it. He was very sincere, very real, and very funny. One of a kind. I don't know where he went undergrad, but recall he had gotten his Masters in History from the University of New Hampshire.

At that time I had no connection whatsoever with New Hampshire, other than it being another New England state – a distant backward "who lives there?" kind of place that got itself called "New England" purely by accident, and not entirely deservedly. It of course never occurred to me that I'd one day raise my kids there.

Anyway, I recall that Charlie's girlfriend was actually *from* New Hampshire, and I can only guess things got more serious because five years later I heard Charlie's unforgettable voice on New Hampshire Public Radio talking politics — he'd become a big player in the State's Republican party. Good for him.

Another memorable co-worker was a tall guy from Argentina. He had the air of an easy-going aristocrat, and I'm sure that was not far from the truth. Pablo was a nice guy, and I suspect a sincere

Christian. I say that primarily because there was one beautiful girl in our circle (one of only two girls I remember working with us) who had asked him to sleep with her — and he had said no. I'm pretty sure Pablo wasn't gay, so considering her remarkable beauty I thought this demonstrated some superhuman powers to which he had somehow gained access.

This story of the botched seduction came not from Pablo himself (who was too much the gentleman to spread such rumors about a lady) but through the omniscient D.C. grapevine. This sort of rejection was likely a first for this good-looking girl, and she had confided to a "friend" the shocking tale of her own defeat. Obviously, unwisely.

About that same time Charlie said to me, completely out of the blue, "Don't do it Mark, OK?" He was referring to that same girl. *"No, Charlie, not me!"*

Then there was the goofy kid with red hair. I say kid, but he was probably twenty-eight. Back then, I thought that was old. This old man had a vicious sense of humor, and one day he convinced all of us youngsters to protest a leftist revolutionary from Central America who was scheduled to speak at Georgetown. "Count me in!"

Matt made signs for all of us that said things like "If you liked Stalin, you'll *LOVE* the FMLN!" He did them very artistically with blood dripping from all the letters *F, M, L,* and *N.* He also led us with his bullhorn in loud '60's-esque chants like, "You started the war, we're gonna end it! You started the war, we're gonna end it!"

We stood outside at a respectful distance. Inside the auditorium, this *Che Geuvara-du-jour* sold Marxist revolution, and 19-year-old girls fresh from the most affluent suburbs in America got wet with the desire to feel his bloody hands on their snow-white bodies. I think it's safe to assume one of them got her wish.

At one point during *Che's* speech, an overweight Mayan woman came outside and gave us two angry thumbs down. She kept her arms stretched out straight in front of her, and pumped her hips up and down to give her disapproving gesture extra effect.

I'm sure she imagined herself holding an AK-47 with which she mowed us all down — and with us the bourgeois Yankee counter-revolution we represented in her mind. I can picture her snarling through clenched teeth "¡Viva la *Revolución!*" as her avenging bullets fly toward the enemies of *The People*, and she repeatedly squats and pumps her hips like that — thinking it will improve her already deadly aim. Really, what a face she had — I'll never forget it. It said clearer than words ever could, "How dare you even *exist!*"

Our protest it seems made quite an impression on Pat Robertson. He actually ran a story about us on national TV as if our gag were real news! Well, I guess it was … in a way.

One day Morton invited me into his office. Even my boss Kevin hardly ever stepped foot in Morton's mahogany and leather abode, let alone peon interns like me.

We talked very briefly about one of the books on his shelves – Whittaker Chambers' *Witness* I think – before he got to the chase: "Mark, I understand you are applying to law schools. Which ones?" I quickly rattled off the long list – *too* quickly, I guess. I could see his mind busily working, trying to keep up with me. "Hmm, Georgetown … I *do* know so-and-so there." It occurred to me then he was not just making conversation, he was trying to see what he could do to help me.

Later he took me out to lunch and the conversation continued. He never flattered me or said anything out of the ordinary; it was just a normal conversation about things I can't recall. It was a few days later that I learned from some of my superiors how unusual it was for Morton to take an employee out to lunch, and that Morton had met privately with me because he thought I'd "make a good candidate." Can you imagine?! Of course Morton, who was a professional judge of these things, was in this case very sorely mistaken. I am not nearly as dependable as he imagined.

I would however like to take a moment to thank Morton for that free lunch, and for his kindness to me. Morton, I'm sorry that I could not become the worthy protégé you somehow mistook me for. I was born a much greater sinner than you.

I should also thank him for introducing me to some pretty big minds. Not merely intellectual introductions (thanks to the many wonderful books he gave me) but also personal ones, thanks to his connections.

Thanks to Morton's organization I got quite easily to meet and shake hands with many men who loved power.

But also with a few who, like me, loved ideas. Especially their own ideas. One such man was Russell Kirk, the self-styled *Abraham* of American intellectual conservatism.

I had already at that time an ancient (that's to say, eight-month-old) love affair with Russell Kirk's books. Meeting the man in the flesh is something I might better never to have done — his books have never been quite as enjoyable since. Though I *did* continue reading them, as you will soon see.

Kirk wasn't a *bad* guy (as were most of the politicos I met), but he wasn't all there. He was a shadow of a man playing a ridiculous role he had invented for himself decades prior. Unfortunately for him and for his soul, he had done so in full view of the world; and then found himself forced to continue on in that part, since so many people expected it of him.

It must be hard being a god, really. Gods need no forgiveness and so, I fear, receive none.

His Victorian-era three-piece suit, his gold pocket watch on a chain, his silk hanky inserted just so, his stilted speech, his affected handshakes. The willful, intensely self-conscious anachronism-ism of it all. Oh, it truly pains me to recall. Especially since I must *also* recall that he lived in a house he had named, in a moment of self-congratulatory delusion, "Piety Hill."

Piety Hill?! Piety doth not name itself, lest it disappear. Hadn't he read Shakespeare?! Of course he had, but somehow this one escaped him:

> *Most dangerous*
> *Is that temptation that doth goad us on*
> *To sin in loving virtue.*
>
> William Shakespeare: <u>Measure for Measure</u>

Poor Mr. Kirk, he's dead now and cannot re-invent himself again. May God have mercy on him ... and on me.

The two of us have much more in common than I care to admit.

Let me take you back to another one of those hob-nobbing events on The Hill. At one, I heard a guy of whom I had never heard, and whose name I didn't bother to notice, speak about his experiences as a POW in Vietnam. He tugged at kitschy heartstrings with his well-rehearsed script, and some in the crowd were moved nearly to tears.

But personally, I thought he was a self-serving phony. His story was true I'm sure and it *was* a powerful one. But that beautiful story had become his wretched whore, and he was pimping her out for personal gain. He was an actor playing a part; hawking a tale that the powerbrokers had told him would sell like hotcakes.

Of course those powerbrokers know their game pretty well, and anyone who wants power would do well to listen to them.

At a different event, another night on The Hill, I heard an Air Force general selling the crowd on the idea of funding SDI – a.k.a. Reagan's "Star Wars." He said it was attainable, and necessary. He quoted some prominent American professor who opposed funding SDI and who had said, "It is absolutely imperative, if we are to maintain the balance of power, that we allow Soviet warheads to reach our country." And then the gray-haired general added, "Well, if you agree with *that* line of thinking, then I guess SDI really *is* a bad idea."

This career military man wasn't a good public speaker at all. He was visibly nervous and awkward — almost bumbling. But in my mind, he seemed to be onto something.

I recalled this bumbling fellow several years later when I read a quote from a dethroned Kremlin official who had said, "It was the threat of SDI that finally broke the back of the Soviet Union." This career Communist then added, "We knew that we had lost the race – that there was no way we could keep up anymore."

So I guess that American professor was right: Reagan's dangerous dreams really *did* screw up the balance of power — just as the learned scholar had predicted.

Another part of my life during those three months in D.C. was Mass at the National Cathedral. I went several Sundays … my first experiences with the Catholic Church. I had felt increasingly drawn to the Church since 1987 when I first discovered William F. Buckley and his friends. Strangely, Bach's *Mass in B Minor* had even more to do with it. Odd that a Lutheran's music could draw a kid from rural New England toward Rome, isn't it?

The National Cathedral sits right on the campus of The Catholic University of America. So that was pretty convenient in a "two birds" kind of way. Because right after Mass I would always wander around the campus hoping to run into a student I had once met very briefly six months prior. Her name was Hope. Really, that *was* her name.

If I did happen to bump into Hope, she would have been hard-pressed to remember me at all. I was surely just one of several fleeting acquaintances she had made that random day in 1988.

But somehow, to me, Hope had become more than just her namesake. She had become the embodiment of Faith and Love as well. And I felt like I had to find her.

Several months after leaving D.C., while in the grips of a burning contagion fever, I even went so far as to write the CUA admissions office from Czechoslovakia trying to locate her. I didn't even know her last name. Only that she was brunette, maybe 21 years old, and named Hope. "Oh, and from Long Island!" I assured in my letter that I was not a dangerous psycho, and implored "the individual reading this right now" to help me.

Of course the frightened school official who had the misfortune to read my insane rambling did not write back. And of course I never found Hope. That letter really should be in a police file somewhere, "just in case," but I'm pretty sure it was just thrown out.

I was getting close in those months to the point of knowing that I'd convert to Catholicism eventually. That had to wait for another year; and another world.

As I said, I had gone to D.C. in January of 1990. And was planning to enter law school in September of that year. My internship was only three months long, so I had six more months to kill before the grueling ordeal of law school. Now what?

Well, I happened to meet a young kid at one of those Capitol Hill shindigs who was recruiting for a brand-new organization called "Education for Democracy." EFD was founded by a Czech-Canadian who thought (for some strange reason or other) that it'd be a great thing to ship a bunch of young North Americans over to the newly free Czechoslovakia ASAP and get them teaching English.

"Sign me up!" quoth I.

Well, sort of. I spoke to the director of EFD and said I'd only go if I could be guaranteed a position in Prague. "No problem, you got it!"

So off I went.

I flew to Paris a week or so before I was due to arrive in Prague, and traveled around Normandy a bit with the time I had left – revisiting old haunts from my year of study abroad. While in Caen, I stopped into an *Armurerie* and admired their guns.

I had always, since the age of eight I guess, been fascinated with guns. But my parents did their best to raise me during the Age of Aquarius, so I'd never touched one. Unless you count the *Red Ryder* BB gun my brother and I secretly bought on the neighborhood black market; and then used to put bloody holes in pretty little songbirds when Mom wasn't home. But that wasn't good enough for me.

Well there in that shop, just a few miles from the D-Day beaches, I found a specimen of *the real thing* with a beautiful wooden stock. It was a single-shot *St. Etienne* .22LR and the price was less than 300 francs ... something like $50. I asked the shop owner about the legalities and learned to my surprise that there really were none. So I bought it.

After Caen, I visited Sophie Deman's family in Lillebonne. Sophie was a fellow student at the University of Rouen in '87, and the bedmate of a friend of mine. She had tried to bed me first, but I had a girlfriend back in the States and was trying at the time to affect some old-fashioned notions about what that meant. So she ended up with John.

Sophie's family lived in *"Le Catillion,"* an impressive old estate of timbers and stucco and solid stone floors. Scattered inside were Roman relics which farmers, over the years, had found on the property — broken Latin tablets, ceramic pottery, and the like. There was also in one room a life-sized granite saint who had been beheaded.

Presumably during the Revolution, when that was the fashion. I'm sure that passionate rabble was disappointed that the stone did not bleed; but I'm just as sure it got its hands on some real flesh that did. *Aux armes, citoyens.*

Someone said that the foundation of *Le Catillion* dated from the time of William the Conqueror, and that there was supposedly some connection to Guillaume himself. But you know how those stories go.

The house actually did not belong to the Demans. They leased it from two old gentlemen-farmers who had inherited the place but could not afford to keep it up. These reclusive old-timers could still be seen putting around on rusty old tractors and tilling the land while listening to Beethoven on their newfangled *Walkmans.*

Much to the delight of Sophie's little brothers I took my new "*carabine*" out into the farmers' fields for a trial run. This would be the first time in my life that I would fire a real gun. But I didn't let anyone know that of course. I tried to act like an old pro the first time I poked a tiny cartridge into the chamber, but honestly I was nervous. I would even say fearful the first time I pulled the trigger.

I suddenly heard a firecracker snap, and it was a little too close for comfort. I looked around quickly, with adrenaline sharpening my vision, and was relieved to realize that everything was fine: I wasn't hurt, nor was anyone else. And I had, in fact, put a little hole in the plastic bottle I had aimed at! I guess years of carefully training BB-gun sights on little chickadee heads had prepared me well for this day.

Sophie's father, a medical doctor, took us on a daylong car tour of *Haute-Normandie.* I had traveled all over France when I studied there, but almost always on trains. Occasionally, as when visiting the D-Day beaches, by bus. But I had never seen France *à l'americaine.*

It was a beautiful and memorable day. We visited several castles … one of which was for sale at a bargain basement price. Really! If you were willing to renovate it, and then pay the taxes and the upkeep, they would practically give it to you.

Mid-day, we stopped beside a stream in the middle of nowhere and set up a picnic. We spread Camembert on hand-split baguettes, ate assorted fruits with our fingers, and shared a cheap bottle of Bordeaux.

Twenty minutes later, a 65-year-old gentleman approached us on foot from the distance. He was dressed in British waxed cotton, and sported a blue and silver *fleur-de-lis* on his brown corduroy collar.

Eventually, he was close enough to speak without raising his voice. He then asked us, in the most elegant French I had ever heard, exactly what the hell we thought we were doing.

Dr. Deman, a lowly member of the bourgeoisie, was visibly deferential. He lowered his head with a guilty half-smile, then carefully explained that he was simply showing the lovely Norman countryside to his American guest, and apologized most sincerely for any intrusion. *"Bonjour Monsieur,"* I interjected, careful not to pronounce those simple words as well as I could.

With that, the old gentleman's face instantly softened and he made it clear, in grandiose literary language, that he was very pleased to leave this little corner of the world at our disposal; and he wished us a very fine day. He then turned and walked away.

We all looked at each other trying not to smile, and subtly lifted our wine glasses in a silent toast.

After Lillebonne, I spent one day and one night in Rouen with the Denis family – the family I lived with during my year there. The *carabine* was a huge hit with the kids there too. Perhaps less so with their mother, but Bibianne always took everything more or less in stride.

I slept in the same attic room that was mine in '87. They still called it "Mark's room," even though one other American student had spent six months there after me. Bibianne told me they never hit it off with the guy and it just hadn't worked out. He moved out shortly after the maid found homosexual porno on the bed when changing his sheets.

I knew *"La Bonne,"* since she worked for the Denis' when I lived there too. Bibianne described how this simple lady who loved rosaries came to her one day in a fluster. And I could just picture the old maid's face as she stammered, *"Oh, Madame, pardonnez–moi. Mais Madame …. Madame. Je viens de trouver quelque chose de … de. Oh Madame, je peux pas vous dire!"**

The kids were all two years older than when I had last seen them, but this was most noticeable in Arnaud's case. When I lived there, he was sixteen and eager to practice his already good English. I think he looked up to me like a big brother, and liked having me around. When I visited though, Arnaud was distant. He seemed bothered to see me.

That may have been because his girlfriend was there. In the afternoon, while I was reading in "my" room, I heard them come upstairs, moan noisily, and then head right back down the stairs. They were in that walk-up attic for a sum total of forty-five seconds, and I'm sure that nobody had even missed them. Not that French parents concern themselves with such things. They really don't.

---

* "Oh Madame, excuse me. But Madame … Madame. I just found something that … that. Oh Madame, I can't even tell you!"

II. Allegro agitato

MY time had finally come to head east. The Iron Curtain had just been punctured five months prior, and I was almost desperate to see what I might find on the other side.

I had already seen most of Western Europe, but absolutely nothing of *The East*. In a perverse way, I desperately hoped that it hadn't changed much in its first few months of freedom.

The train ride from Paris to the Czech border took all day. I had already spent hundreds of happy hours in European trains, so this was no big deal and nothing new to me.

At one point, late in the afternoon, the train stopped with a bang. And then we sat. And sat. And sat. Finally, I heard something going on ahead and I stuck my head out the window. And I'll never forget what I saw: An antique locomotive straight out of *Dr. Zhivago* heading toward me, replete with a big red star on the front — preparing to attach itself to our rail car so that it could drag us behind the dark side of the curtain from whence it came. *"Oh, this is too good to be true!"*

A cloud of dirty smoke then rose over everything and I had to remind myself that everything was fine: The Commies really *had* lost once and for all.

The doors opened brusquely and loudly, and a greasy woman of about forty-five boarded the train. She sported an ill-fitting and wrinkled uniform, and an expression of blank hostility. She worked from seat to seat, checking tickets and "papers." When she got to me, she grabbed my blue passport and barked at me loudly in a completely unintelligible language.

I was tired, so it took me a couple of seconds before I interpreted her aggressive gestures to mean that I had better hurry up and get my filthy American feet off of that seat in front of me. "Oh, I'm sorry, I hadn't realized they were there," I mumbled quietly ... trying not to further inflame the situation by speaking English to her but not knowing what else to do.

She scribbled a note on her pad, slapped my passport back at me, and continued down the aisle.

Such was my initiation into life behind the Iron Curtain. A curtain which now had gaping holes in it, but which certainly had not disappeared overnight. Much, I must confess, to my relief and delight.*

When I got to Prague I somehow found my way to my destination — a grand baroque chateau on the outskirts of the city. It was a patrician estate which the Communists had stolen from its rightful owners forty years prior, and which now belonged to the Ministry of Education. I found myself in the company of two other foreigners who had just arrived, and who had not yet been assigned to their new teaching posts. We were shown to a well-lit room filled with beds, and then left to mill around wondering what might come next.

"Uh, Hi, Sir, I'm the guy who got promised a position right here in Prague. So ... when do I start?"

The emotionless Czech who seemed to be in charge of communicating with this motley group of visitors had no idea what I was talking about, nor who had made that promise. Neither did he seem terribly concerned to find out. He simply glided out of the room and left me alone with my new friends.

I spent the next two hours conversing awkwardly with a somewhat chubby Canadian redhead twice my age — searching with

---

* This was, of course, a pretty tame initiation. I'm fortunate she did not search my luggage and find the disassembled target rifle in there. Then I might have ended up with some even more unusual material to share with you. How many Americans can write about their first night in an East Bloc prison?!

difficulty for common ground. Meanwhile, his dark-haired traveling companion (a skinny youngster like myself) brooded suspiciously in silence.

At one point, the conversation finally took a hopeful turn when the redhead mentioned something I cared about: classical music. When I expressed my admiration for Karajan's Beethoven he replied, "Well, he was terrible to work for. A Nazi really. At least that's what my friends who knew him *personally* always said." With the word "personally" the Canadian pursed his lips, raised his eyebrows, and turned his head far aside. And his companion's brooding seemed to intensify.

I began to get a better sense of exactly whom I'd be bunking with for God-knows-how-long and, though I'd had a few gay friends in college, I must confess that I wasn't entirely pleased with the situation.

Journal entry from August 29, 1990

"J'ai découvert que tout le malheur des hommes vient d'une seule chose, qui est de ne savoir pas demeurer en repos, dans une chambre."

Blaise Pascal: *Pensées*.

Rough translation: "I have discovered that all the unhappiness of men comes from one thing: Not knowing how to sit quietly in a room, all by oneself."

I decided to head the hell out of the Ministry for a while, and killed some time sightseeing in Prague. While wandering around Old Town Square (which was not nearly as busy as I hear it is these days) I sensed a very important commotion going on. Though the square had several dozen people walking randomly through it, a large tightly packed crowd of three dozen or so made itself obvious, and moved very clearly straight toward me. When this group was still fifty feet away, I caught a clear view of the individual around whom it was centered – Margaret Thatcher.

I could hardly believe my eyes as I saw her walking nearly straight toward me. I stood stunned for a couple of seconds before I thought to pull out my Nikon and prepare myself. As I did, I noticed two eyes focus instantly on my black camera, and then quickly but subtly look elsewhere for more dangerous threats. She was surrounded by bodyguards. Most of whom wore ill-fitting and dated suits — which clearly identified them as Czechs. Only one of them looked positively dapper, and smiled broadly at my camera as I snapped my first shot. He was clearly British, and very relaxed. The rest were stone-faced and serious, and clearly knew that there was a lot riding on them doing their jobs very well. Which of course they did.

It occurred to me a few hours later as I lay trying to sleep in that surrealistic bedroom that these well-trained bodyguards, who were not young by any means, had almost certainly cut their teeth protecting Communist bigwigs. And here they were protecting the sworn enemy of these men on her triumphal tour! Those bigshots had finally been beaten … and by a woman no less!

Shame, and eternal shame. Nothing but shame.

Maggie was welcomed to Prague while I was there as part of the victorious triumvirate of which Reagan and the Pope were also members. This victory march infuriated virtually every single academic and intellectual that I knew, since they saw all three of these characters as the incarnation of evil on earth. Of course they did not believe in the possibility of Incarnation *or* of Evil, but that did not prevent them from ascribing such metaphysical distinctions to these three.

A tiny minority of these intellectuals were highly intelligent and honest Marxists who saw the collapse of Communism very lucently as a defeat, and a treacherous betrayal. It was *Götterdämmerung* — the twilight of their gods. A *very* bitter pill to swallow.

Most of them, however, were less intelligent and less honest. They were fuzzy thinkers who felt pangs of inner conflict when The Wall fell. They wanted suddenly to claim that this was the culmination of all of their dreams ... that the Cold War had finally ended! They were keen to add that there was of course no victor and no loser — that it was just finally over. That the bad guys on both sides of The Curtain had lost, and that we now could all, finally, move on in a bright new direction.

They wanted to share in the Czechs' joy, and share in the credit for bringing that joy about. They too wanted to travel to Prague and to be hailed as heroes ... but the Czechs had no idea who they were and didn't give a damn.

So instead of feting these Western intellectuals for their sophisticated sentiments and noble intentions, the Czechs threw grand parties for Maggie, welcomed the Pope with open arms, spoke glowingly of Ronald Reagan, and committed other such infuriatingly impious acts nearly every day.

Oh, 1990 was a very difficult year for that generation of Westerners for whom America had been the root of all evil, and for whom the Cold War had just been one big misunderstanding.

These minds have since moved on and managed to forget about the confusion and pain of 1990. They have now found new bugaboos to occupy themselves with. Actually, they manage to find another new one every six hours or so.

As long as they can keep playing this distracting game, they will never have to examine their own consciences and explore the lessons of modern history with open eyes. They will never have to figure out which side they were rooting for during the Cold War. Nor will they have to look into their own souls and worry about where that soul might be headed in another decade or two.

I hope at least one of them reading my words will be brave enough to sit quietly in a room, all alone, and ask these tough questions. But I'm certainly not banking on that.

The next morning, back at the Ministry of Smartness, our Czech keeper told me matter-of-factly that there was no job for me in Prague, but that I'd be shipped off to Brno instead. That it would be my honor to teach employees of the prestigious arms manufacturer *Česká Zbrojovka*. (Had *he* checked my luggage?!)

I said, essentially, "Well, I don't have much choice, do I? I mean, here I am in Prague without a flight ticket home — what am I going to do?" I resolved to make the best of it in Brno.

There were two positions there: I had one and the other was to be taken by my talkative Canadian friend. *"Hmm, I wonder where his quiet little buddy will go?"*

The next morning I was told coldly that there had been a change of plans. I was not going to Brno after all, but to *Hodonín*.

"What the hell is *Hodonín*?" Well obviously I was about to find out.

Honestly, I have no recollection whatsoever of how I got to that little industrial city in the wilderness of Southeastern Moravia. I can't even recall my first day there.

I just remember being there, like I had always been there. I had been sent to the gulag decades prior for being naïve enough to demand a position in Prague. And to think that a promise made by some do-gooder in the free world had any bearing on things over here.

I had really wanted to see the East Bloc experience — but I didn't want to actually *live* it! At least not as authentically as *this!*

I feel differently now – I'm glad I had that experience. But at the time I felt like Kundera's *Joke* was on me.

"Kamaráde! Jak se maš, dnes? Eh?!"

"What did he say? I think I heard the word 'Comrade,' but the rest is just nonsense."

No, Mark, you misunderstood everything. He called you a "friend." And he knows that you are definitely *not* a Comrade.

You, however, *cannot* be so sure about him.

Journal Entry from June 15, 1990

"The moral state of mankind fills me with dismay and horrors. The abyss of Hell itself seems to yawn before me. I must act, think, and feel according to the exigencies of this tremendous reason."

Edmund Burke: Reflections on the Revolution in France.

Hodonín's main claim to fame is that it is the birthplace of Czechoslovakia's first president, Tomáš Masaryk, who helped craft the new nation from scratch out of the ashes of the Austro-Hungarian Empire after World War One.

Masaryk truly was a great and thoughtful man in the mold of his friend Woodrow Wilson. Only wiser, and probably smarter too.

Of course he was *not* a Communist. On the contrary, he once wrote a philosophical treatise critical of utopianism in general, and Marxism in particular. So of course this town's one and only true mark of honor was viewed as an unforgivable sin by the authorities.

Perhaps that's one of the reasons those authorities blighted this place with a massive electric generator that burned "brown" (i.e. sulphurous and toxic) coal. They blighted it further with inhuman concrete apartment buildings that make the projects in The Bronx look positively inspired.*

These human cages were all about a dozen stories tall, and for the most part exactly the same. They usually sprouted up in bunches of at least four, sometimes dozens. Very occasionally one would pop up all on its own, standing alone like a concrete tree some farmer had left in his barren field "just because."

Inside these massive cages, every little rat had his own five-hundred square feet of space. Not really "his" space of course, but the one the State generously allowed his body to occupy – provided he didn't make trouble. "You know, there *is* a waiting list for this flat."

The elevators in these gray monsters were too narrow to handle more than two rats at a time. So before he could get to the safety of his own compartment, a rat did occasionally have to wait downstairs in the uncomfortable presence of another rat he'd never spoken with — and would rather not.

I, of course, was one of those rats. And I had company. Free cages were hard to come by, so I had to share mine with Jill, a girl from Canada who had also been sent to the gulag for some infraction or other. Thankfully, I did not find her attractive in the least — that made things much less complicated.

Our cellblock had only two rooms and a bath. One of those two rooms was the bedroom of course, so the "lady" got that. I slept in the kitchen. Or the dining room. Or the living room. Whatever you want to call it, OK?! The 12'x10' room with white concrete walls and

---

* Hodonín was not unusually blessed in this regard – these gray buildings cropped up everywhere, throughout the East Bloc, in the 1950's and 1960's. Occasionally a 500-year-old church or a synagogue had to make way for them. Progress does have its demands you know!

a kitchen sink. The one that Jill had to walk through to get to her own private space.

I did at least have a window of my own, so I could look out on the next concrete building, or another one if I preferred. Or yet another! It's always nice to have choices.

One warm night, sleeping with my window cracked open, I woke up choking to death. My lungs felt invisible hands squeezing them, and my tongue burned with the taste of metallic toxins.

I later learned that when the sun goes down, Prague's demand for electricity goes up — so the brown coal gets shoveled fast and furious down in far away Hodonín. Conveniently, the darkness of night hides the noxious orange cloud that descends on the city when the winds decide they are too tired to carry it away to Austria.

It would be entirely reasonable to assume that nothing beautiful could come out of a place like this, but I have learned that beauty is resilient. Defying reason and all odds, human souls that loved other human souls and thirsted for God somehow survived in these inhuman concrete cubicles. These souls were in the minority, I'll grant you that, but that even a single one could breathe in these conditions seems like a minor miracle to me.

I got to know several such kindred spirits in Hodonín. One dwelt in a woman named Jarka, a student of mine. She lived of course, like me, in a concrete cage. Only hers was on the outskirts of the city and had *two* bedrooms! She shared it with her husband and three kids.

Jarka had a kind face, but it showed signs of wear beyond her thirty-something years.

Often, after class, she would do unexpected things for me. Like hand me a whole currant cake, still in the pan, which she had baked that morning. Before long, she essentially invited me into her family. And I gladly accepted the invitation.

Jarka was always very anxious to talk about God with me, and looked to me for direction in this regard as if I were some authority on the subject. I felt like a terrible phony, but I did my best for her. I mean, I was glad to say I *believed* in God (after many dark years of pretending that I did not) but I still wasn't exactly sure what He was or what I was or how this all fit together.

Of course I didn't share my uncertainties with Jarka at all. It was clear my rôle was to be her rock, and I didn't want to let the nice lady down.

Her husband had a good heart too, but he tried hard to hide that fact. He claimed to be an atheist, and enjoyed repeating the mantra that "God is for foolish old grandmothers" as if he had never said it before, and as if that brilliant observation had just come to him for the first time. He was also always anxious, in the same breath, to let you know that he had been an irreproachable anti-communist even in the bad old days.

Josef was not an unusual type in the Czechoslovakia of that day: a reasonably intelligent man who claimed to hate the Communists, but who had internalized 99% of what they had taught him for the past forty years. Which is to say of course for his entire life.

"An ignorant man, who is not fool enough to meddle with his clock, is however sufficiently confident to think he can safely take to pieces, and put together at his pleasure, a moral machine of another guise, importance, and complexity, composed of far other wheels, and springs, and balances, and counter-acting and co-operating powers ... Their delusive good intention is no sort of excuse for their presumption."
Edmund Burke: Reflections on the Revolution in France.

"Man must adore something, and, having denied God, he will find his deity somewhere much lower than the angels."
Russell Kirk: The Conservative Mind.

Josef's political education started very early it seems. As I looked through the books in Jarka's tiny cramped home, I found one that looked very much in size and color like the Dr. Seuss books I had loved as a toddler. It was clearly a bedtime "Read-to-Me" kind of book, with colorful pictures and several large-font sentences on each page.

Only this one was different. It was the story of a four-year-old Czech boy named Jiři and his friendship with Vlasta, a kind-hearted Russian soldier of nineteen or so. It told the story of how Vlasta had driven his tank *so far* just to come and help the Czechs. "Mommy, he came here so we can live in *Peace!*" The boy loved his new friend like a big brother. The grateful lad offered the young soldier a single red flower, and got a yellow one in return. A white dove floated above their heads like a halo the two of them shared. On the opposite page, a sweet and gentle "Poem of Peace."

I'm sure you think I am making this up; but I promise you, I am not.

I suppose a parent could choose not to read bedtime stories like these to their toddlers, but the indoctrination became mandatory in kindergarten. There, five-year-old kids wore red scarves and sang beautifully musical songs glorifying Lenin, who, in the context of these little moldable minds, might be considered the "George Washington" of Communist history lessons. But He is of course more fully understood as the Christ of Communist catechism.

This sort of indoctrination continued from kindergarten on, every year, straight though until high school graduation. Schoolteachers were the parish priests of this 20th century religion, and tolerating aposty amongst their ranks was not an option — the stakes were far too high.

And lest a child forget these important lessons during the long summer break, they were re-enforced even more memorably at summer camp. There, separated from the unreliable bedtime influence of parents, children learned to associate the glories of nature and of sleeping in cabins with proletariat unity and dreams of human perfectibility.

It seems miraculous to me that a single one of these kids grew up to participate in the anti-communist revolution of 1989, but somehow half a million of them did. As I said, beauty is remarkably resilient. And ugliness not as powerful as it seems.

I had three teaching positions in Hodonín. Two at local factories, where I taught foremen and managers, and another at the town hall, where dozens of schoolteachers came to practice their English with me and on me. It was the latter position that gave me insight into the souls of the East's "guardians of youth." It was not a pretty sight.

A few of these teachers were already proficient in English, but most were not. They had taught Russian – not a great stretch for any Slav. (Although it uses a different alphabet, Russian is quite similar to Czech. In fact, many words and phrases are virtually identical.)

My class was in big demand because this horde of Russian teachers knew that the "new authorities in Prague" had given English precedence over Russian in classrooms, and they did not want to find themselves out of work. They needed to make themselves useful to the regime … as they ably had done for decades already. "Welcome to the new boss!"

Some of them were clearly having trouble adjusting smoothly to post-Communist life. I met many who tried to change their colors like a chameleon and to blend into the re-emerging fabric of Czech life. They feigned excitement with "the wonderful new changes" and spoke glowingly about "market reforms" and "freedom of the press."

I think the habits of parroting the words of Prague authorities had become ingrained, and they had shifted gears reflexively when "the authorities" started speaking a new language. But beyond that habitual impulse, I think they also feared retribution — and had climbed vocally on the new bandwagon in a desperate effort to save their skin.

Incredibly though (despite the clamoring of a vocal minority who wanted "justice") no retribution ever came. This was partly because the new president, Václav Havel (who had himself been abused and imprisoned by the Communists for many years) spoke with his inimitable eloquence about the value of forgiveness and the futility of vengeance.

It was also because virtually nobody in the country was entirely free of guilt. Almost all hands had at least a little spot of blood on them, or held hands that did.

Though some teachers had this miraculous conversion experience I just talked about, many of the ones I taught were completely unchanged by the Velvet Revolution – other than discovering a sudden desire to learn English.

One of these unrepentants once asked me pointedly, "What sort of person goes to university in America?" I knew very well what she was getting at but I dodged her implication with, "Well, pretty much anyone who wants to."

She wasn't going to let me go that easy though, and kept pressing with, "Don't you have to be one of *The Rich?*" I shot back, "Actually, no, you don't. And you shouldn't always look at things through a Marxist lens."

She seemed surprised I had cut to the chase so succinctly and replied pseudo-apologetically, "Oh, but that's all we were taught!"

I just shrugged and bit my tongue, because it would have taken things a bit too far had I replied, "Don't you mean all you *taught?*"

As far as this Marxism-wearied business, I've found it to be a very common problem among teachers. Naturally, the ideological watchdogs paid special attention to teachers and frequently gave them political "education" classes as well as I.Q. tests (that's "ideological quotient"). Though most of the teachers hated that aspect of their work and are glad that the Commies are out, enough garbage sank in to make them oddly superstitious, pessimistic, and generally unhappy. The illness is common among university professors in the USA, too, but there it is self-inflicted.

Journal Entry from July 1, 1990

Many Utopians haven't rejected God, but rather rebel against Him to spite Him (i.e. "If you won't give us a perfect world, we'll show you!")

This is all very heroic, but I suspect there are a lot of heroes in Hell.

Of all the dozens of teachers I taught, one stands in my memory more vividly than any other. Her name was Vera, and she was a tall blonde of about fifty. She had intelligent blue eyes, and looked like she had probably been attractive at one point in her life — but her rotten soul had fixed that years ago. I disliked her the first time I saw her, and that feeling only grew stronger the better I got to know her.

Her English was impeccable — *far* better than that of any other student in my class. In fact, it was *so* good there was hardly any need for her to be there. But I suspect she was there for other reasons.

During every class, and after every class, she engaged me somewhat aggressively in banter. She would smile, and try to feign playfulness and camaraderie, but it was an act. I smelled a rat.

One day, after I had known her for about a month, she asked me if I'd like to come over to her place to see some collection or other. She did so in such a creative way that "no" was not an option.

Vera lived in an old pre-War building downtown which was not entirely unattractive from the outside. It was no architectural marvel, but a far cry for the sort of building I (and most people) lived in. When I got inside, I noticed that her apartment looked very different from most I had seen. It was decorated more expensively, and with items that seemed to indicate a penchant for travel in the decadent West. She asked if I'd like a drink, and I said, "Sure." She then pulled out a flat box, and opened it. It was full of those tiny little booze bottles you'd see in Western airplanes.

For someone who has never lived in the East, it's impossible to understand how incredibly rare and precious these Western liquors were. There were at least a dozen choices in that box (Chivas Regal, Remy Martin, Tanguerey, etc) and multiples of several choices. Vera had obviously been doing very well for herself.

I foolishly reached for the only Chivas in there and perceived a very subtle wince in her face. So I said, "You know, thanks, but I'll pass. Thank you anyway though."

We talked about I know not what for about five minutes before the conversation suddenly became memorable. She asked me casually, "So what exactly did you do in Washington?" I remember that question like it was yesterday. I remember exactly how I was sitting and everything that was around me. I felt the blood leave my face, and I felt a little bit ill.

I was *sure* I had never told her, nor anyone else in Hodonín, about my short stint in D.C.

"Holy crap, I really *am* in one of Kundera's novels!" And the joke was still on me.

Let me ask you something: Why are you reading this? Yes, I'm talking to you.

Are you with me now? Paying attention?

What I want to know is why you would spend some of your life, and perhaps some of your even more precious dollars, so that you could spy into someone else's supposed "memories" ... which may or may not be true. How would you know? Why should you care? Does any of this matter?

Let me be bold and take this a step further: Has it occurred to you that I can't hear you? So why am I asking you questions? And why are you feeling a little uncomfortable right now? Are you feeling guilty that you didn't stop to figure out any of the answers to the questions you'd been asked before just forging ahead and leaving them all unanswered?

OK, relax. You may return to your illusion now. I just wanted you to think about all of that for a moment.

Journal Entry from July 9, 1990

"Man never rushes forward so confidently, it would sometimes seem, as when he is on the very brink of the abyss."

Irving Babbitt

Inefficiency and a lack of individual responsibility were both huge parts of life in the East. I'd like to illustrate those two things separately, which is very hard to do. But here goes:

Inefficiency:

1) The hot water in all of those cubicles I told you about was provided from a single, centralized hot water heater. I never knew that until there was a notice posted on the one door every single rat had to open stating that the water heater was being repaired, and that our entire neighborhood (thousands of people) would be without hot water for the next two days or so. "Wow, is that possible?!" I had always remarked that the water blasting out of the faucet (the pressure was like nothing I'd ever seen) was WAY too hot – literally boiling – and I always wondered how one might adjust that. I mean, the water was so damn hot I couldn't even use it to shave with – and that's about the only time I actually WANT really hot water. But this was *so* hot that the razor would burn my skin after I had rinsed it off. And the pressure was so intense that, if I wasn't very careful, scalding water would blast into the sink and then shoot straight back up into my face and/or all over the bathroom. To make it worse, the sink had two separate faucets (one hot, one cold) so it wasn't like I could mix some cold in there to get the temperature I was looking for. Unless I did by carefully making a big deep puddle in the bowl, and I always hated doing that. That sink was my daily nemesis. But baths were nice and, though I was never a bather in the States, I took to it there out of necessity. The bath had one of those showerheads on a flexible cord, and there was nowhere to hang it and no shower curtain anyway so showers were pretty much an awkward sitting affair. Might as well take a good hot bath and fill it to the brim. Often I'd open the drain while the hot water was gushing out of that underwater faucet to give myself a constant circulation of water – kind of a poor man's jet-tub. I *did* enjoy that.

2) Phones had neither "long distance block" nor detailed billing. A factory or a school would simply get a phone bill every month and have to pay it, not knowing why it was so big or who had made calls and to whom. (I assume the secret police knew those details, but if so that was a secret.) I learned about this mystery billing issue later when I was teaching at the university in Brno (I know, I'll get to that later) and my department director spoke to all of us and explained that suddenly the phone bill had gone through the roof and he wanted to know who was making international calls on our lines. (I swear, it wasn't me! I'm almost sure it was the other American teaching there – a shifty Deconstructionist from Seattle. I'll get to him later too.) It's a little off-subject (inefficiency, remember?) but while I'm talking about phones let me tell you another story from Hodonín. Shortly after my encounter with Vera, I began to feel a little bit paranoid. Can you blame me? I imagined that, though Havel had cut off their funding, the secret police ("StB") were busily working without pay, as if on autopilot, collecting files on everyone just in case the Communists managed to get the reins back. I wasn't worried for myself ... I knew I'd end up safe back in the States. But what about Jarka? Was I creating a problem for her? I calmed myself with the assurance that there was *NO WAY* they were getting the reins back – I was sure of that. Well right after that incident with Vera I discovered, by accident, a phone booth that was broken. No, the phone worked, it was just the slot that took money didn't. Or just didn't care that you hadn't put any money in. I direct dialed anywhere in the world and it was perfectly happy to connect my call and keep it connected for as long as I wanted to speak. I started using that phone to call people in the States whenever I felt like it. I used it almost every day for at least a week. Then one day when I was speaking to a friend in Connecticut and said something about "these fucking Commies" the phone immediately went dead. It would not work any more, whether

you put coins in it or you didn't. Now before you go thinking I really *AM* paranoid, let me say I'm sure – really sure – that was just a weird coincidence. But it is a *really* weird one, huh?

Oh yes, I just remembered, I was planning on talking about individual responsibility too. But I guess I already have.

The physical environments that I taught in gave me insights into the spiritual environments I had been plopped into. At the factories, I taught in barren conference rooms with canvas walls and vinyl flooring. To get to these rooms, I'd have to pass through a narrow corridor and by a guard desk to assure that I was not a confused slave who had taken a wrong turn on his way to the trenches. When I entered the room, I would first face a large rectangle of un-faded canvas where a portrait of president Husák — Moscow's man in Prague — had hung since the 1970's; his glum mug shot having been removed just a few months before my arrival.

High up on the wall behind where I stood teaching, both in the factories and the town hall, was a familiar sight I saw nearly everywhere I went: a two-foot-wide pattern of un-faded fabric in the shape of a hammer-and-sickle.

I would like to have hung a cross up there in its place, but that surely would have troubled my students greatly. And the teacher too, who had no business representing a symbol that important to the middle-aged blank slates who came to my classes.

Now that I'm writing about life in Hodonín, I'm remembering a little more about my incarceration there. I still don't remember the first day but I do remember Petr, the kind man who had made all the arrangements for me and Jill. He had that flat waiting for us, and did his best to make us comfortable.

He even gave each of us brand-new bicycles so we could get around town easier. He also gave us chains and locks – and was very careful to explain how they worked. He spoke virtually no English, and at that point I spoke no Czech at all, but we somehow managed to communicate just fine.

Once day Petr invited me to play tennis with him. I really had no idea how to play but I certainly was not going to turn down his kind offer. He handed me a racket and we walked from his office to a beautiful red clay court. I didn't know much about courts either, but I knew this was a nice one. Which is to say, of course, quite out-of-place in Hodonín.

Like many Czechs, Petr was a great tennis player. I'm sure it was painful for him to keep running out of bounds to retrieve my wild shots, and to have so few volleys extend beyond three hits. But he was always kind to me and never once looked even the least bit put-off. He was really a good guy.

I never understood exactly what his job was, but I think it must have been something like a municipal administrator. Whatever it was, I know he performed it with compassion, skill, and dedication.

That bike he had given me was a life-safer. Without it I would have jumped out of my cell window and made a mess in front of the entrance. The other rats would have had to walk around my stinking corpse before getting to the safety of their cages, and I'm sure that would have annoyed them. So I guess my bike had some value from their perspective as well.

Anyway, I mention the psychological importance of the bike because one day I went into the basement of our apartment building, where everyone kept their bikes locked up, and found that both mine and Jill's had been vandalized. Some of their moving parts had been removed and stolen, but most others had simply been kicked and destroyed.

I walked the long walk to Petr's office and tried to explain to him what had happened. I don't think we got any further than getting him to understand there was some problem with my bike. He jumped into his little car and motioned for me to hop in. His car was a new Škoda *Favorit* (nice by East Bloc standards) and being a car buff I looked around with interest at all its clean but primitive controls while he drove us back to my place.

I'll never forget Petr's face when he looked at our bikes. It was a combination of anger, disappointment, pain, and ... most evidently ... shame. He stared at those bikes for a long time before looking back at me and trying to tell me that he was sorry without knowing the word for that.

He had both bikes fixed by the next day, but mine was never quite the same. It wobbled when I got up to speed, and it was more difficult to pedal. It still was my workhorse though, and helped keep me somewhat sane during those months.

About two weeks after this incident, one of my factory-worker students showed me a front-page article in a local paper, which he had proudly translated into English for me. In the middle of the page was a picture of my mangled bike with the caption, "Bike After the Tornado!" It was a long, full-page article about what had happened, written by my friend Petr.

It was an emotional and impassioned diatribe. Directed, very obviously, toward the individuals responsible for this deed. And perhaps more generally toward the town that had bred them. A public shaming of sorts for everyone to share.

This incredibly long piece contained all sorts of factual errors. For example, it said that Jill and I did not understand why we even *needed* locks for our bikes, and that nothing like this had ever happened to us before.

In point of fact, *exactly* the same thing had happened to me two years prior when I left my new ten-speed locked up outside a college dormitory in Connecticut. I had also seen dozens of bicycle skeletons in Manhattan that barely gave a hint to the full working body that once lay there.

Theft, violence, and youthful indiscretion were hardly the exclusive domain of the East, but that's what this article seemed to imply.

Another error in the article was the statement that Jill and I had come to Hodonín voluntarily. Well, not exactly. Petr spoke almost poetically (and more than a little melodramatically) about how we had left our comfortable lives in North America to help the poor people of Hodonín, "and *this* is how we have thanked them!"

The whole thing was pretty overblown and kind of pathetic. But it came from the heart of a kind man who was hurt to see that his kindness had been trampled, and embarrassed that his hometown had abused the first Westerners he had ever befriended. Reading this article gave me deeper insight into the heart and mind of a friend that I could only speak with in gestures.

As I got to know Jarka better, and discussed religion with her more frequently, I began to understand the complicated inner struggle she found herself in. Genetically, a Catholic. But raised in a Communist country that mocked and persecuted any belief whatsoever. Sleeping with, and raising three kids with, a man who did the same. And now, as the veil of the Iron Curtain was lifting, her best friend was suddenly trying to sell her on the enlightenment of Seventh Day Adventism. This friend was the first who had ever dared discuss God with Jarka, and it awakened something deep in her heart. She was intrigued, and interested, and had some very sincere belief that somehow she *had* been missing something important her entire life. And now this trusted friend was telling her exactly what this something was. But somehow, something wasn't quite right about this Seventh Day stuff. Jarka really wanted to believe *something*, but felt a strange compulsion to find a reason not to believe *that*. She knew she was too unschooled to stand up to her friend's well-rehearsed untruths, and feared that she would soon fall victim to them if something were not done quickly.

Poor Jarka was terribly confused by it all. And desperately hoped that this new American friend, who'd been raised in a free country, in "One Nation Under God," could somehow make it all work for her and tell her what to do with her life and her soul.

My God, what a huge responsibility you placed on these unworthy shoulders.

I was at that point not yet a Catholic, but a fellow traveler at the least. So I made some effort to push Jarka in the direction her ancestors had traveled for many centuries. It seemed like a safe bet.

I encouraged her to go to Mass with me, which was something I had yet to do in Hodonín. She agreed, since she felt that was now a "safe" thing to do.

She explained that if she had gone six months earlier, she might have lost her job. You see, she explained, the town hall (where, you recall, I taught) maintained a list of churchgoers. If you were just a "foolish old grandmother," there was no harm being on that list. But if you were a thirty-something mother of three, the price of admission was far too high. At the very least, you'd be limiting your prospects for advancement at work. At the worst, you'd be turning your insecure children into public laughingstock, and limiting *their* prospects for advancement at school and beyond. Something no mother could endure.

Most troubling of all, to me, was her revelation that priests often helped to maintain these lists. Either because they were bribed to do so, blackmailed into it, or, in a few cases, because they really felt that was the right thing to do for the good of *The State*.

Though I wasn't sure whether to believe this tale of widespread complicity among priests, it clearly was the sanctioned "word on the street" in Czechoslovakia.* And that rumor accomplished exactly what it was supposed to: keeping the vast majority of children away from any religion that might compete with the one they picked up in school. The one that taught them that salvation first came to the world in 1917 in a town once called *St. Petersburg*, but which was now more virtuously known as *Leningrad* — the Bethlehem of Communism.

Jarka *did* attend Mass with me in a little yellow church, and did manage to fend off her friend's American-imported certainty about the hell-bound evils of everything Roman.

Or I should say Jarka fended them off at least as long as she had this real-life American around ... I sadly haven't kept up with her since.

I'm sorry about that Jarka. I hope you're well.

And if you now agree with your friend and think that I tried to lead you to the devil's yellow palace, that's OK. I still love you. *Theos ein agape.*

Petr made sure I was paid well, and it was from him I would collect my monthly salary of 3400 crowns, paid in a big colorful stack of cash. As I recall the exchange rate in those days was thirty-two crowns to the dollar, so that was just a little more than one hundred dollars per month.

---

* I'm sorry to report that I have recently learned this rumor was all too true. There were many secret police agents and collaborators within the Church, operating within a Church structure called Pacem in terris ("Peace on earth"). Several prominent Catholic officials were outed as Judases in the '90's, including the dean of the Theology Faculty in Prague. Sadder still, for me, is the fact that these men were never held accountable by the Church for their treacherous betrayal of Christ's sheep, and continue to wield influence in this veil of tears. My Church can do what it will. I leave these men to heaven, and to their thorns.

I never lacked for money, and could do or buy just about anything I wanted. Of course I was paid a salary that normally would support an entire family, so that shouldn't be surprising. I had only myself to worry about.

I made an effort to spend all of my crowns before the month was through, and it wasn't easy. I bought classical CD's for one hundred crowns apiece, superb hiking boots for three hundred, a backpack and a nylon tent for about the same. Some of those items would serve me well on my many hitchhiking adventures.

I ate out almost all the time too. The restaurant near my "home" served virtually nothing but Weiner Schnitzel, dumplings, and beer. The last item was the only one I enjoyed at all, so I remember the price ... eight crowns. So I guess I wasn't paid all that well after all ... only four-hundred-something beers per month?!

I don't mean to imply I drank heavily in those days, I did not. A beer or so per day, occasionally an evening with three or four. The only time I remember getting drunk in Hodonín was the night I was invited to a wine tasting in the nearby countryside with a group of five Czechs of about my age.

At about sunset, our host drove us into a field toward a wooden door with no house behind it. He parked, removed the padlock from that door, and opened it to reveal a stone stairwell leading to a large cave below the vines. He led us all down the stairs with his flashlight and seated us around a beefy wooden table while he lit candles all around.

It was then that his mannerisms transformed; and I realized that I was a privileged witness to an ancient peasant ritual.

He smiled as he served everyone a small glass of white wine straight from the cask, and handed each one off with a flourish. Once everyone was served, our proud host stood at the head of the table with his legs spread far. He then crossed his arms, smiled, and looked askance at the nothing on his right. And then the nothing on his left. His face beamed all the while and he pushed his chest out as far as he could manage with his arms crossed high on top of it.

He then said some loud incantation in Czech that I could not understand, and expanded his arms toward us with a silent gesture that I could. It said, "Please, my friends, drink!" So drink I did.

I first realized that I was drunk on the ride home as I sat in the back seat beside a twenty-two-year-old girl who was seven months pregnant. I suddenly discovered, to my horror, that she looked irresistible: I needed to grab her swollen body and make it mine.

She *was* quite pretty, but she was also outrageously pregnant with another man's child! Drunk as I was, I had the sense to know that my desires were evil and to be suppressed at any cost. I also knew that only extreme drunkenness could allow thoughts *this vile* to enter a man's consciousness. I was seriously incapacitated, and I knew it. A little voice spoke to me and said, "Man, you are *smashed!* So take it easy! Tomorrow this wickedness will be a thing of the past — just between you and me. Nobody else will ever know what's going through your head right now, I promise. Just sit tight … you'll be back in your cage soon!"

I listened intently to this sensible voice and squeezed my knees hard with both hands. I closed my eyes so I would not be temped to look at her, and I prayed we'd get back before I did or said anything unforgivable.

Twenty minutes later I stumbled into the safety of my cage, collapsed on the bed, and spun myself to sleep.

Journal entry from October 23, 1990

"I committed fornication against Thee, and all around me thus fornicating there echoed 'Well done! Well done!' For the friendship

of this world is fornication against Thee; and 'Well done! Well done!' echoes on till one is ashamed not to be thus a man."

St. Augustine: <u>Confessions.</u>

When I woke I was not spinning any more. No, the elephant standing on my forehead precluded that. He was holding me down in place ably with his many tons centered on a few square inches just north of my eyebrows. The risen sun blasted my pupils like a million-candlepower lighthouse that I could not turn off even if I closed my eyes. *Ah, the pain!!*

It would be an understatement to say that this was not a convenient morning to be hung-over. In two hours I was due to give a lecture at the local technical school. I had to educate these poor prisoners on the glories of the U.S. Constitution — as if I were a legal scholar or something! I had in fact just read the whole thing through, for the first time, two months prior.

So I was unqualified, ill-prepared, and in mortal pain. A very bad combination — which was about to get even worse.

The teacher who had invited me to speak had a pretty limited command of the English language, and had told me to show up at "ten half," which I interpreted to mean 10:30. What she *meant* to say was "half ten," which is still nonsensical. But as I had just learned in German (and would later learn in Czech) *"halb zehn"* (or *půl desáté*) would mean 9:30. *That's* when I was supposed to be there, and ironically at *"halb zehn"* I was still lying in my bed, sipping bitter tap water, and listening to an Austrian radio broadcast in an effort to passively learn German.

I lay there for a long while wondering if I'd ever get my brain back; and then heard the radio announce importantly, *"Der Ziet, in fünf Sekunde, ist zehn heur.* **Bong!** *Zehn huer. Die Österreichicher Rundfunk senden Nachrichten."*

"OK, I got that. It says it's ten o'clock. I'd better head over to that school now and wing it. Then I can go back to sleep!"

The bike ride to the school took less than ten minutes, so I actually got there "early" — like about 10:15. When I walked through the school's main entrance, the teacher who had invited me ran up to me, sweating and panting, and looking even worse than I felt. I could not understand her garbled words, but clearly there was some sort of crisis going on.

"Fear not, dear damsel, I come bearing *The Constitution of the United States of America!* All will be well!"

She led me nearly at a run down a wide hallway, toward the lecture hall, and then I walked into its expanse. 300 heads turned, and 600 eyes glared at me in total silence.

"Oh. My head really hurts you know. And I think I'm gonna puke."

I trudged up to the front of the room and tried to smile, even though that tightened the sensitive skin on my pounding forehead. Then I turned to face a massive crowd, and launched into my charade as best I could.

"Yes, well, the separation of powers … *yadda yadda yadda*."

"Now, the judiciary interprets … *yadda yadda yadda*."

Why are you all staring at me like that? Can you tell I'm hung over? Did someone tell you about last night? I didn't touch her leg or anything, did I? My God, word travels fast around these parts, huh?! I gotta get out of this hellhole!

"Uh, any questions? OK, class dismissed!"

Eighteen years after that "lecture" I still feel like I owe an apology to the poor souls who sat through that nonsense, and to the Founding Fathers who drafted the inspired document I so publicly abused. I'm sorry. I really am.

After I slept off my hangover I put some genuine effort into learning German by picking up the sturdy little Bible I had bought at *Stefansplaz* in Vienna, and copying David's Psalms into my journal:

Herr, erhebe dich, mein Gott, bring mir hilfe!

Dies Irae

Flickering flames blown furious
Scorch one born for better.
Wind whips
but will not cool
the mortal burns that never die.

Hopeless howls unheard in Heaven
Still echo through the selfish universe.

"Echo, Echo, Echo
Burn, Burn, Burn
Die, Die, Die."

Did, but never will.

Over the next few days, as I contemplated my own depraved state, I tried to project myself into a happier future. I tried to imagine myself un-haunted by the demons that had possessed me since an overdose of testosterone had first encouraged me to lust after my sisters in Christ. Demons that smiled and goaded me on and clapped me on the back and called me a hero once I got to that supermarket of flesh called college.

I bemoaned the shocking fact, which I could scarcely believe even as it became inescapable, that countless pretty girls lusted for me too. That the fields lay so ripe before me, and the fruits so easy to harvest.

Many men would take this as a blessing, but for me it became a curse. I wished to become so revolting that no girl would ever want to touch me. That I'd be forced to abandon all hope in this life before I had to abandon the same in the next.

I'd become a monk. "Yes, *there's* true happiness on this earth." I seriously contemplated such a life. I think I even prayed about it. I guess I must have, because the Holy Spirit came to me one day as I lay in my cell block there in Hodonín and said to me clearly and calmly, *"No, not you young man."*

Laying aside those dreams of solitary bliss at God's bidding I thought, *"Well then, what?!"* I conjured in my mind an idea of marital bliss, where all the sexual energy now spilling out of me would be funneled cleanly into a vessel of pure love in God's sight and with God's blessing. I wondered if such a thing were truly possible, and dared to envisage it. I almost could, but not quite. I wasn't sold on the idea, but I hadn't discounted it either.

I said another prayer inspired by David's Psalms, and a vision appeared before me. No, not a dagger ... something much more beautiful.

I then jumped up from my knees, grabbed my journal, and wrote on that day, the twenty-fourth of June, 1990:

"I held her Christian face between my hands and kissed it – reverently."

And exactly eight and half years after I wrote those words I did just that. Because she had just said yes.

Praisèd be God, and not our strength for it.

Lately Meeting Juliet

Surely she hasn't seen what I have seen
I thought as I approached down the darkened hall.
Portraits on the wall had seen I was sure
but they had problems of their own.
Strangely as the distance closed
eyes opened and saw eyes.
Pure in brilliant dimness.
Darkness unreflected.
No reproaches no denial.
Just Truth and Light and Life.
All there ever was.
I loved her.
Not for anything but
I loved her.
Pure as those eyes,
Mirrors of redemption.
Looking back I might have
Wondered worried disbelieved.
But in truth there was no struggle.
No forgetting forgiveness or ignorance.
The moment transcended all that.
Nothing but truth, light, life.
All there ever was.
Pure and good.
I didn't sense her lips as
We kissed beneath her great ancestors.
The moment transcended all that.
We lived dead with dull joy
and timeless courage.
Here was forever
forever here.
Truth, light, life.
All there ever was.
Darkness unreflected.

Well that was a nice diversion, wasn't it? But sorry, this story must now return to the darkness of 1990, and the dirtiness of Hodonín.

Journal entry from July 9, 1990

I'd like to consider myself a traditionalist, but the links are broken. So I lunge desperately through the vapidity, stretching, grasping: and earning that unwanted title – Reactionary. Of course the one benefit of this situation is that I'm compelled to grab the strongest link of all.

I guess industrial backwaters exist everywhere, and that it's unfair of me to associate so much of Hodonín's unpleasantness with the East Bloc experience. But I'm sorry, I can't help it. When I recall that place, it's the uniquely Eastern details that come back to me; and it's those details that define it for me.

Let me try to take you through just one hour in my life there: it's a sunny morning in May, 1990.

I wake up on a brown bed/couch with a single white sheet below me, and another one over me. A yellowed lace curtain of stiff coarse fabric hangs just beside me and diffuses only partially the sunlight filling my little room. My face is close to the window and I notice again that the curtain smells (as does everything in this town when you really pay attention) of petroleum or smoke or some other toxin I can't quite place. I sit up in bed, wrinkling the thin loose sheet beneath me, and squint as I look out the window through the tiny round holes in the curtain and through the fine layer of coal dust which coats the glass outside. I see a building just like mine about fifty yards away, and a couple of smaller buildings nearby too. I don't see any people anywhere, though I know thousands of them live within earshot of where I sit. They must all be hiding, like me, behind smelly curtains. A few faded East Bloc cars, all at least twenty years old, rest on the pavement below me. But most of the pavement is bare … sort of like an asphalt lawn that runs between my building and those nearby.

I turn and put my feet on the hard concrete floor, which is covered only by a thin gray industrial carpet. I shuffle six feet from my bed over to the small gas range, and remove with a clang the thin tin teakettle. I take one step to my left and I'm at the sink. I stick the neck of the kettle around the faucet and turn on the water, which instantly blasts out with such force that it nearly knocks the kettle out of my hand and shoots water all around, making a mess.

I look over at the closed bedroom door just six feet to my right. I wonder whether my roommate is sleeping in there, or whether she has already left. I don't really care, as long as I don't have to see her. "I'll try to get out of here soon just in case she *is* in there."

While the water heats up, I take a few steps toward the entrance/exit to our little flat, and duck into the bathroom. I turn on the bathroom sink's hot water … carefully. A cloud of steam instantly rises, and I toss a washcloth under the flow. I shut off the water and pick up the washcloth — which burns my hands uncomfortably. I allow it to air cool a little before touching it to my face, and then attempt to shave with a dull razor. It doesn't work, though the blade is brand new: I just bought it yesterday. With a few less whiskers and a few more bloody nicks than I started with, I head back to the kitchen to finish making my coffee. I shake a few dozen coffee beans out of a 4"x4" brown plastic package, grind them up, and dump the grounds into a coffee mug. I pour boiling water onto the grounds, give them a stir, and then give the mug a hard whack on the countertop to try to send the grounds bottomward. Soon, I am ingesting my morning drug … a luxury I feel very fortunate to enjoy here in the gulag. I wouldn't have expected life to be this good.

I head down the small entry hallway, past the bathroom, and open the door quietly to exit our apartment. The windowless 10'x 8' space before me is lit only by a single 40-watt bulb, and my eyes have trouble adjusting. I *can* see well enough though to see that nobody else is waiting for the elevator, and am relieved. I press the button, and soon slide the iron bars aside so that I can enter the 3'x4' box that will take me seven floors down to the street.

I leave my building via a flimsy glass-and-metal door, which rattles shut behind me, and I step onto the asphalt lawn before me. I take a deep breath of polluted air, and can just barely detect a whiff of freedom that must have blown here from the Vienna woods eighty miles to my south.

The sun shines brightly on my face. Scientifically, I know this is the same sun I've known my whole life: the one that has shone on me in Vermont, Florida, the Alps, the Greek Islands, and a thousand other places that I do not call home. But there's much more to life than science, and in my heart I know that no, this is not the same sun at all.

I walk past a baby-blue Trabant and study its faded plastic resin exterior and whisper a jesting guess to myself: "1970." It's a pointless game I've started to enjoy. Every car-obsessed man here knows that you can only guess the age of a Trabant by its condition, but that you will never be sure of your answer: They were identically produced from 1963-1990 without a single change … cosmetic or otherwise.

I walk down the dusty street and see my first human being of the day: a moderately overweight man of about fifty dressed in dusty gray-blue overalls and sporting a dusty cap to match. He trudges with his back slightly bent and his face down, as if he were carrying something heavy. One of his fists is clenched around a small white paper bag, and the other is clenched around a red pencil. He lifts his eyes to notice me then quickly puts his head back down. As he walks past me I get the distinct impression he is trying to study me in his peripheral vision without averting his eyes from the dusty sidewalk in front of him. "A Westerner!" he's probably thinking. "Perhaps a spy."

As I walk down the street into the older part of town, I see a few more people about. The stucco buildings around me are no longer bare-concrete gray, like those in my neighborhood. They are all painted a certain shade of yellow. But they are still gray nonetheless, since they are covered with a fine layer of dust and dirt, and have obviously been neither cleaned nor painted for many decades. It all gives one the feeling of a ghost town, and the few lifeless people trudging about do nothing to diminish that impression.

I turn a corner and find myself in the direct line of fire of a huge tank. This happens to me here every day, so I'm not startled. It's a vintage Soviet T-34, in pristine condition. The retired vehicle's beefy tracks rest, somewhat crookedly, on two unequal concrete blocks. This antique weapon sports a fresh glossy coat of dark green paint and a bright red star on its turret, and I can't help but notice that this paint is much fresher and cleaner than any I see on any other building or vehicle in town. I wonder … *"who saw to that?"*

As I dodge past the tank, I hear a raspy whining noise behind me. I turn to look just as I am passed by a young man of about my age riding a Jawa motorcycle. I notice how remarkably similar this new Czech bike looks to the old '65 Honda my Dad rode when I was a kid: the same primitive drum brakes, the same thick spoke wheels, the same half-melon headlamp, the same flat, contourless seat. I also notice that the air I'm breathing, which was never pleasant, takes a turn for the worse as I find myself walking though the cloud of dark smoke this hooligan has left behind him. But nonetheless, I find myself envying him. The 350cc two-stroke engine propels him very quickly down the nearly deserted road, and I'm sure he experiences a euphoric sensation of freedom and superiority as he flies past a humble, earth-bound pedestrian. I'm also sure he indulged in that guilty pleasure on sunny May days in years past too. I wonder, *"Did anything change for this guy six months ago? Does he know that he just blew past a U.S. citizen? The first to live in Hodonín since … the beginning of time?"*

"I doubt he knows," I think to myself. *"But if he does know, I hope that was his best flyby yet."*

My cellmate and I didn't talk any more than necessary, but one day out of the blue Jill shared with me that her grandmother back in Alberta was, and always had been, "a Socialist." I didn't tell her that we had something in common after all, because I didn't really *want* to have anything in common with her. And also because I could tell that, unlike me, she had not broken with her family's Leftist heritage. I didn't want to start an argument with someone I had to share a toilet with. So rather than have a far-too-honest conversation with her, I kept my questions to myself: *"Has the gulag begun to weaken her? Why else would she tell me something like that?"* I suspect that the harsh realities of Hodonín were seriously challenging her faith — just as they were shaping mine.

Journal Entry from May 28, 1990

A system where only the rich are powerful is far better than one where only the powerful are rich.

I received an early birthday card of sorts from my parents. It always was a nice diversion to get mail from the West, and I got quite a lot of it delivered to my cell block in Hodonín: from family in Connecticut, Massachusetts, and Florida; and from friends in D.C., Seattle, and Rouen.

Reading my parents' card gave me a smile that lasted all of three seconds, and then I forgot all about it. Until a few weeks later when I was speaking to my Mom on the phone and she asked, "Were you able to change that cash OK?"

Umm, huh?

I then learned that she had stuck a twenty dollar bill inside that card ... not knowing that the secret police were still steaming open all letters coming from the West, and then skillfully re-sealing them to leave nary a trace of their meddling. But this American cash — more than a postal worker would earn in an entire week — was clearly too good to resist. Especially since Havel was trying to make things hard on honest snoops, and money was especially tight right then.

This little anecdote illustrates a point that I was constantly trying, unsuccessfully, to make when speaking to people in the West. Everyone I knew thought that the Iron Curtain had fallen and that the Cold War was over. I would almost shout at them over transatlantic phone lines, "Look, Havel is president now, fine. But that's it! Nothing else has changed over here!"

Although I was a bit hysterical on the subject at the time, I was not very far off either.

For forty years a massive machine had been built, and that machine gained a new driver (albeit an unwilling one) in 1990. But that big ol' machine kept right on chugging along. You can't stop a freight train in an instant just by putting on the brakes. Nor can you swipe clean layers and layers of corrupt bureaucracy just because you suddenly decide that you don't want to take it anymore.

I think we'd all be wise to remember the lessons of 1990, and to see clearly the rampant corruption that still rules in the East today. We should remember this before creating any new bureaucracy to "solve" our problems. We should remember this before we expand the powers of bureaucracies that exist already. Because when we finally realize what we have done to ourselves and to our country, no amount of wishing will make it any better. We're screwed.

Sorry, I know this tale of life in Hodonín has been quite dark. But my life there *did* have its lighter, humorous aspects. Well, come to think of it, most of them are only funny in retrospect. This is one of my favorites:

In my first weeks there, I found myself constantly speaking with people with whom I shared no common language whatsoever. I would speak either English or French (it made no difference at all) and I'd use lots of hand gestures to get my point across. And people would inevitably smile broadly at me and nod their heads furiously as if to say, "Yes, yes, I understand!"

However, only one word crossed their lips, over and over, and it was spoken with gusto: *"No, no, NO!"* These mixed signals of an affirmative nod and a negative exclamation filled me with angst and confusion.

It took me much longer than it should have to figure out that "no" is the Czech word for "yes." Even after I did come to that realization I found it impossible to entirely re-program my mind and accept that someone really could mean something very kind and reaffirming when they are yelling "NO!" at you. My angst never left me entirely, and even once I could speak a bit of Czech myself that weird word still sometimes disarmed me. *Yes, Ja, Da, Oui, Si* … those all work just fine. But *NO?!* What the hell is wrong with these people?!*

Besides my friend Petr and my enemies in the secret police, there were other State officials who took great interest in little ol' me. One of these was, I believe, from the *Ministry of Culture* or some such thing. That anybody in a "Ministry of Culture" had any idea how to

---

* In case you're interested in technicalities, I'll tell you that the real word for yes is "ano," but this is usually shortened to a simple "no." Doesn't that bug you … at least a little?

get hold of me, or any interest in getting hold of me, shows, I think, the intrusive efficiency of the system the Communists had created.

Lots of people knew lots of things about foreigners living in the country. Foreigners who, in any Western country, would have received all of the anonymity and slight regard that they truly deserved.

But my Western passport alone was enough to turn me into a VIP whom the authorities felt obligated to educate, entertain, and, of course, keep an eye on.

To be kind, I'll say I do think this imperative went beyond and through the omniscient paranoia of Communism. It was also tied up in the Czechs' natural extroversion, their national pride, and their innate kindness.

With all of the above prerogatives in mind, this keeper of culture invited me to a Moravian Folk Festival in the rural outskirts of Hodonín soon after I arrived there.

It was a singularly erotic experience, and one I later learned that (for some odd reason or other) had been heartily endorsed and funded by the Communist authorities since the fifties. So I was apparently not the first foreigner aroused at the State's expense with the sights and sounds of ancient Czech mating rituals.

I appreciated very quickly that Czech folk songs are incredibly beautiful; and human in the most unaffected, simple way. They are all heart, with just a little bit of loin thrown in – not to imply that there's necessarily a disconnect between these two. The head should kindly leave itself at the door please.

As the dulcimer hammers out its rhythms and timeless melodies, the sexes play their own eternal roles without a hint of intellectual interference. Men put their hands on their hips, expand their chests, and survey the beautiful scene before them with glee and heartfelt appreciation for the passing pleasures which dance so temporarily before them.

Fertile maidens in colorful flowing skirts spin themselves dizzy and yip out exclamations of excitement and joy which pierce the male heart to the core with desire and wonder.

Everyone has their heaven-given role, and nobody thinks for an instant that they don't like the one they've been assigned. As *The Bartered Bride's* opening chorus exclaims so heartily,

> *Proč bychom se nětěšili,*
> *když nám Pán Bůh zdraví dá,*
> *jenom ten jest v pravdě šťasten,*
> *kdo života užívá.**

This is not some licentious *carpe diem,* nor a sophisticated *savoir vivre.* It's just the joy of living, pure and unadulterated. Something I had never truly witnessed until I saw Czech peasants dancing.

And the fact that they happened to be dancing at their perverted master's bidding didn't change a thing. It really didn't.

I only worked four days per week, and I left Hodonín every one of those long weekends to avoid making a bloody mess below my window. Prague was a bit far, but in less than two hours I could be in Vienna, and I went there often to fill my lungs with Western air and my heart with timeless music. The *Musikverein* became my Olympus, and I would sit in her cheapest seats and drink her Ambrosia ... which flowed just as freely up there as in the pricey seats below.

Getting to Vienna was an interesting affair. As I said, I was paid well ... but not in "hard currency" of course. In the West to my south, my Czech crowns were nothing but colorful monopoly money. So as soon as I crossed the border I was living on saved dollars in an American bank account ... of which I had only a couple thousand.

To conserve those dollars for important things (like tickets to

---

* Why should we be unhappy when the Lord grants us health? Only he is truly happy who lives life while he still has it.

the Vienna Philharmonic) I hitch-hiked. My simple routine was this: take the ten-minute train ride to Břeclav, then hike five minutes across the border into Austria, then hold up a sign and wait. I had to pass customs twice on foot: once to leave the East, and once to enter the West. More than a few times I noticed the Czech officials do a doubletake at my American passport … *"you don't see one of these every day!"* They would sometimes look at the passport and then carefully at my face … *"hmm, no horns in the picture or the real thing. That's odd! But they do match, so … guess I'm supposed to let him go!"*

The Austrian officials were much less impressed with blue passports, and did not usually even glance at my picture or my face. *"Ja Ja, geh."* Or more often simply "sank you" and a wave of the hand.

So a short train ride to the border, a short walk across that border, and then I'd stand for a while with a cardboard sign labeled "*WIEN.*" Sometimes I'd have to wait for a full hour, but it usually did not take that long. Most of the time Austrians picked me up, which was nice … more opportunity to practice my German. And their accent is so much nicer than that of the Prussian Hun … it actually makes German sound (dare I say it?) beautiful!

I recall one Volkswagen driver exclaiming, "Your German is very good for an American!" I thanked him for the backhanded compliment as I thought, *"Well of course! I've been working on it for two whole months now!"* The truth is German was coming to me quickly and easily, simply from listening to Austrian radio in my cellblock. Czech was going to take more effort than I was willing to give it.

Once I got to Vienna, that Athens of breathing marble and pissing poodles, I'd invariably hop on a tram for a run around the Ring and a refresher tour. *"Yes!"* Vienna is my favorite concert hall in the world. I did not, and would not, call it my favorite city. Although I love that place dearly, I would not want to live there. Because *nobody* lives there. Not really anyway.

I remember once looking both ways before crossing a Viennese street (my Mom taught me that trick once) and having a perfectly clear view of a completely deserted street, I strode confidently across that street in the direction of a middle-aged gentleman dressed in green and gray tweeds. As I approached, the kind man smiled at me with an open mouth and wide-open eyes. He pointed helpfully at the red pedestrian glowing from a pole behind me, indicating that one should not cross the street right now. I smiled at him trying hard to feign ignorance and guilt as I replied, *"Oh, danke schön!"*

So for my weekend jaunts Vienna had top billing. Then Prague. Then Bratislava. Once I rode an antique locomotive all the way out to the Soviet/Ukrainian border, which scared the hell out of me and made me anxious to get back to the comforts of my cellblock in Hodonín.

Strangely, I almost never visited nearby Brno. Maybe it was too close? Or maybe it reminded me of the chatty Canadian who had slipped my Czech handler a twenty-dollar bill to assure that his boy-toy would not be shipped off to the gulag — and that I would instead? There certainly was nothing *else* wrong with this city of 400,000 … it's a wonderful place with rolling hills, beautiful architecture, and *nearly* world-class music. It's not Vienna or Prague, but located somewhat between these cultural giants it's the next best thing.

Brno is the capital of Moravia, and the second largest city in what is now the Czech Republic. It had been the home of Milan Kundera and scores of less important smart people. Gregor Mendel for example.

During the Thirty Years' War, Brno's hills and fortress walls helped give it the proud distinction of having been the only city to successfully defend itself against the Swedes.

As we all know hills and walls became less daunting as military technology progressed. So for the past century or two this town's political fortunes have been determined far outside its forgotten gates.

In one respect, Brno reminded me of Rouen: a fairly large city with a grand medieval history ... doomed forever to play second fiddle. But Brno has the benefit of being two full hours from Prague and Vienna, whereas Rouen is only one hour north of Paris. That's a little too close for comfort when you're the little guy.

After I'd been in Hodonín for a couple of months, I received an invitation to attend an event at the English Department of Masaryk University in Brno.

I assume that every foreigner teaching English in Moravia (there were already dozens of us scattered here and there) had been invited. So I had received the invitation simply because I was an American. Not because I had studied photographed reproductions of the history books that Shakespeare had read, and had written a thesis analyzing how those pages found their way into the Bard's plays. Nobody knew that, and nobody cared.

The university building I went to was large and architecturally pleasing. Simple, but not primitive. I believe (though this is purely my own speculation) that the man who designed that building believed in God, and did not think himself terribly important. Architects of that ilk went extinct sometime around 1925, so my best guess is this place was built right before then.

I walked up a fifteen-foot-wide stairwell with worn stone treads, toward a large lecture hall buzzing with English conversation. How bizarre this sounded to me ... a crowd of people speaking English! I was drawn magnetically into the room, and lost myself there. I wandered around smiling, and then latched onto the first individual I found not already engrossed in conversation. Her name was Jana, and she had a very kind, ordinary face. Slightly shy, probably in her mid-thirties. She was a local Czech working toward an assistant professorship in English.

Early in our conversation she asked me where I was teaching.

When I said "Hodonín" a look of blank sympathy came over her face. After a pregnant pause she said, "let me introduce you to someone."

She led me over to a crowd of eight gathered around a small thin man with long snow-white hair and a permanent smile. He was talking a mile a minute, pausing only to blink or occasionally to listen carefully to someone's comment before wittily using that comment to launch a new joke.

Jana and I stood there somewhat awkwardly, as people always do when they've invited themselves to stand in the midst of a lively conversation that started before they got there.

The white-haired man we were listening to was Don Sparling, the newly appointed head of the English Department. He had an obvious and strong Ontario accent, which I found very pleasant to the ear. As he buzzed along to the chuckles of all around, he glanced over at Jana and made his smile just a little bigger to acknowledge her presence. She smiled back and nodded, with evident respect for the man mixed with an appreciation for his humor.

Occasionally, Don would throw a Czech phrase into the conversation with the ease of a native — which he practically was. He had, at that point, been living in Brno for 21 years — settling here almost by accident after falling in love with a Czech girl in 1969 after doing graduate studies at Oxford.

Improbably, they were still married. And had two young Czechs with Canadian passports crammed into their apartment with them.

How Don thrived in Brno, and never lost that smile in those dark years right after the Russian tanks rolled in, is still a mystery to me. He's a remarkable character.*

---

* Occasionally I have wondered: is it possible Don had been a Communist himself? Why else would a brilliant Canadian choose to live through that hell? *Et tu Brute?* But no, I'm convinced that he really did simply fall in love. First, with a girl; then, with a land. And he never left either of them. Bravo, my friend. Bravissimo.

I know the "conversation" I just described sounds a little like an egocentric monologue. But no, not at all. Though Don was doing most of the talking, he was fully engaged with everyone there, including Jana once she arrived. Not yet with me, but he would soon take steps to fix that.

One of his colleagues made some comment or other, and Don approached the speaker quickly, touched him on the arm with his left hand, and said, "Yes, yes, yes!" Then in almost the same movement he approached my new friend with an extended right hand and said, "Hello there, Jana!" That was of course her cue to introduce me, which she took very ably.

"Well, well, welcome to Brno! Are you having a good time?" I told him that yes, I was, and that I hadn't realized how much I missed hearing a crowd of people speaking English until now. "Well that's great, so glad to hear!"

I now wonder if it was in that instant that Don decided to offer me a job, or if it took him a little longer. I'm inclined to think the former: he was an incredibly fast decision-maker.

I don't think hiring me was the *best* decision he ever made, but I sure am glad he made it. If he hadn't, I probably would have shown up at Boston University Law School in September 1990 and been miserable. Instead, I had the honor of continuing my love affair with Moravia. A love which, improbable as it seems, had been born in that dirty little city I once referred to as *the gulag*.

There were many people living behind the Iron Curtain who had been virtually silent for decades. When they met me, I somehow became their confessor, and they had to speak. Sadly, most of their stories are now lost to me forever. However, I do have a few of them to share with you:

CATALOGUE

Tom's father was imprisoned for one and a half years for saying that the Soviet occupation was a Soviet occupation.

Oscar Viktorin was sentenced to five years hard labor in the late '50's for publishing anti-gov't pamphlets. He escaped from his camp, however, hid in the woods for several days, and walked to Austria. He then went to Hamburg where he took a boat to Australia. He lived there for several years and then went to Alaska. He's now a US citizen.

Hanna told me that her uncle injured one of his eyes very seriously – he was going to lose it. At the hospital the administrators said, "I'm sorry, we can't help you. You're not a member of The Party, are you?" He joined the Party on the spot and his eye was saved.*

One of my students received threatening calls from the police because he received mailings from the BBC. This seems incredibly trivial when compared to the incidents above, but is it?

Jiří, my oldest student, used to be a teacher of History and Czech. But his father had been a preacher once, and so Jiří was "reassigned" to work as a manual laborer in a factory. He's still there.

Speaking to a friend about book collecting I learned that many of the most precious old books were lost or damaged in their confiscation from Church libraries.

Jarka was sternly reprimanded for exclaiming "Oh my God!" while in front of a State Council. She feared they would take her

---

* There's another note I put down here a few months later: "But it wasn't so easy to join the Party." And that's the truth of it I think. Many people had very creative covers for the moral compromises they had made, and this story sounds unlikely to me. It surely has a grain of truth in it: I'm sure his eye was saved thanks to his Party membership. But I suspect that membership pre-dated his injury.

family's apartment as a punishment. The council had mercy, however, and forgave her.

The Communists built a 4-lane highway right through the middle of old Bratislava, tearing down everything in its path – including the most beautiful synagogue in Central Europe. The highway just barely missed the city's large Cathedral, so masses must now compete with the din of 18-wheelers.

Journal entry from July 5, 1990

I hate destruction – and want to destroy it.

One evening near the end of my stint in Hodonín, Petr invited me to join him and a few friends out in the countryside for "*špekáček.*" I had no idea what that meant, but the way he kept repeating the word (looking me intently in the eyes) I could tell this meant a lot to him. I could also tell he assumed it meant a lot to me; that he felt it was something the two of us already shared.

We drove down a dirt road through some woods just as it was getting dark, and parked in a small clearing. Petr and another guy got quickly to work building a campfire, which was soon roaring. We then all sat as close to the fire as we could without getting burned, and Petr produced a five-foot-long stick with a fat sausage stuck on one end. He thrust it toward me and said with even greater intensity as the fire reflected in his eyes, "*špekáček!*"

Once everyone had a stick in their hands and a sausage in the fire, Petr started to sing in a high, tremolo tenor. His baritone friend joined in and soon everyone, except for me, was singing songs that, though in Czech, sounded an awful lot like the kinds of songs American cowboys used to sing when there was such a thing.

So *that's* what *"špekáček"* is all about, and why he felt I needed to see this: He needed me to know that we were brothers.

The culture of the American West permeates the Czech lands, and it has for a very long time. Somehow that story of a life away on the range in a new untamed land speaks directly to the Czech soul in a profound way that's hard to comprehend. These "cowboy songs" have been sung around Czech campfires for a hundred years.

But the connection between the Czech and American soul goes far beyond the culture of the Wild West and, most odd of all, it's a two way street. It's easy to try to explain this bizarre connection between a big powerful nation and a tiny powerless one as having sprung from the deep friendship between Wilson and Mararyk, and their co-operation in founding Czechoslovakia as a new nation in 1918: a brotherhood of young nations in a world of old ones. The problem with that explanation is that these spiritual ties pre-date the founding of Czechoslovakia by a very long time. Czechs living in the Austro-Hungarian Empire, with no expectation that they would one day found a new nation of self-determination, still felt connected to the spirit of America.

When one says something like that it's hard not to be misunderstood. It helps I think to remember I'm talking about the 19th century. So of course I am not referencing American popular culture, which did not vanquish the world of thought until much later. But neither am I talking about the American dream of material wealth — which *did* have currency in other parts of the world in the 1800's: Ireland and Italy for example. Those nations have connections with America which are very different and much more insular: They are largely about money and/or the lack thereof. The Czech-American connection goes deeper than that and, I would like to repeat, the connection goes both ways.

There was never a mass-migration of Czechs heading off to "make it" in America. Perhaps that's because the hard-working Czechs were never destitute. But I like to think it's because most of them loved their land too much to leave it. I don't know about now, but in 1990 they loved their land the same way Americans did when they could sing, "This land is your land, this land is my land." That idea has sounded hollow to American ears for many decades, but it spoke directly to the Czechs when I was there. They felt a connection to that idea even when, technically, the Czech lands were *not* theirs.

I think the spiritual connection to land, which is all but lost in America today, is a big part of the mystery of Czech-American friendship.

I'd hate to tell the Czechs what has become of us; I'd hate to tell them what they are probably becoming.

There are many examples of Czechs enriching American culture: I think they often understand our better selves more clearly than we do. I think Dvořák, whose best symphony is "From The New World," can be called the musical equivalent of de Toqueville. Listen to his 9th again and try to forget that you already know the tune; try to hear what he is saying about us. You might be embarrassed when you realize that he is talking about things we have forgotten. The four characters in his "American Quartet" also have a conversation that sounds oddly familiar in a distant, nostalgic sort of way.

There are other bits of Czech musical culture that are 100% Czech, and yet still somehow speak directly to the American soul. We can thank Mahler for one of those connections; since, in 1909, during his brief reign at the Metropolitan Opera, he had the courage and foresight to stage Smetana's *Bartered Bride* — which was completely unknown to American audiences at that time.

The story does feature a brief appearance of "A Bear from the American West," but other than that little cameo this opera is straight from the Czech soil and the Czech soul. It is a strange tale revolving around the bizarre concept of brokered marriages; and it is set to unfamiliar and quintessentially Slavic rhythms.

But beneath all that, it's really a beautiful story about the vagaries of life, the primacy of love, and the courageous pursuit of one's dreams. The Americans naturally went wild for it.

Let's follow these musical winds across the Atlantic again, this time in an easterly direction: Besides those cowboy ballads I mentioned, there are many other examples of American music and spirituality bleeding into Czech culture. One of these that served the Czechs well in an hour of need is the African-American spiritual, "We Shall Overcome," which is actually sung to the tune of an old Latin hymn written just about the time Africans were first being shackled and loaded into wooden boats. That's to say, about the first time there *was* such a thing as an African-American.

We Shall Overcome. In November and December of 1989, during those intense weeks of the Velvet Revolution, hundreds of thousands of people sang this haunting music in unison in Wenceslas Square, both in English and in Czech. With special emphasis on that glorious phrase *I do believe.*

This musical message of hope and faith in the face of seemingly insurmountable odds gave these protesters the strength to carry on until the evil powers-that-be finally gave up hope themselves.

Ironically, the song had been introduced and popularized here thanks to the globetrotting efforts of Pete Seeger, who had been a member of CPUSA* from 1942-1950.

---

* i.e. the "Communist Party of the USA." Yes, there is such a thing, and for a while it was quite influential in this country—until the Soviet Union stopped funding it with a $3,000,000 annual grant. Gorbachev cut off this subsidy in 1989 because the leaders of CPUSA had spoken out against Glasnost and Perestroika, and Gorby didn't appreciate these uppity Americans suddenly thinking that they had a right to break away from the Kremlin's party line. Didn't Dan Rather tell you that story? No? Well, I guess he thought it wasn't very interesting.

In the Prague of 1964, Seeger was stunned to find himself being whistled and booed by crowds of freedom-obsessed Czechs when he spoke out against the Vietnam War.

But those same Czechs loved, learned, and never forgot Seeger's rendition of *We Shall Overcome*.

History is full of such rich ironies … if only you are willing to see them.

Another odd historical tidbit for you: Nearly all of the most important dates in 20th century Czech history end in the numeral eight. So the Velvet Revolution was *clearly* a year late. Here's why:

In 1918, "Czechoslovakia" was born.

In 1938, the British and French threw the Czechs to the wolves at a meeting in Munich – in their infamous "peace deal" with Hitler.

In 1948, Czech Communists (with Stalin's "fraternal" support) seized power in Prague.

And in '68, the Russians sent the tanks in to make sure that the Czechs understood who their masters *really* were, and to make sure that the Iron Curtain did not drift eastward. It was really supposed to move in the *other* direction. *Why don't those damn Czechs understand that?!*

Although none of these historical events are truly the subject of this book, they all influence it. The last one, in particular, is one that I'd like to take a moment to explore in more detail.

It's one I heard about often, since many of the Czechs I befriended in 1990 remembered 1968 all too well. They remembered hearing those tanks, smelling their exhaust fumes, and seeing them drive down roads intended for cars; and they remembered the sinking feeling that all was lost. They remembered the nearly two decades of "normalization" that followed, and the surrealistic nature of life without truth. They remembered old high school pals turning on them and telling the secret police about the "traitorous" activities they had engaged in: Like removing street signs, and using the Russian they had been forced to learn in school to give young tank drivers directions. Directions that led them back toward Moscow instead of toward Prague.

When the tanks, despite these bad directions, rolled into Wenceslas Square, they were met with weeping, shouting, and fighting. Crowds of young Czechs jumped on top of those tanks and tried to stop them. They tried to reason with the frightened young Russians driving them.

Failing to convince these fellow Slavs to disobey orders and face court-martial, they attempted to light the tanks on fire with gasoline bombs. They set up blockades with disabled trams and busses. Blockades the tanks pushed quite easily aside.

Some young Czechs fought with their bodies in any way they could. They whacked long wooden poles against the tanks as if that might help. Others fought with their poetic minds, and blindfolded stone statues so that they would not see what was happening to their homeland.

While this lopsided battle raged in the streets, Czech broadcasting continually ran Smetana's patriotic music on a loop until Russian troops broke into the studios and shut it off.

When the battle was long lost, and the secret police were still busy interrogating anyone who had dared to defy the tanks, a young man named Jan poured gasoline over his head, kneeled quietly beside his nation's patron saint, and struck a match.

What was happening in '68 that prompted those tanks to roll? What were young Czechs up to while American youth were fighting the Vietcong, fighting each other, and fighting *The Greatest Generation* — while shamelessly claiming that distinction for themselves?

Young Czechs were doing a lot of things. They were listening to The Beatles. They were getting naked. They were reading banned literature. They were *writing* literature that would later *also* be banned.

The beautiful promises of *Prague Spring* began on January 5, 1968, when a kind-faced Communist (yes, really) named Alexander Dubček was appointed head of the Party. Dubček immediately launched reforms aimed at creating "socialism with a human face," including reforms that allowed for freedom of the press and freedom of expression — two very dangerous things when you are dealing with people as literate and as intelligent as the Czechs.

Young Czechs ran with these new freedoms with all their hearts, and often in ways that died-in-the-wool Marxists like Dubček did not agree with. But Dubček did absolutely nothing to suppress them … which of course made Moscow very nervous. The Russians had continual talks with this questionable upstart, seeking reassurance that he was not taking Czechoslovakia down the rebellious road that Hungary had travelled in '56. Dubček earnestly assured them that he was not; and he pledged, sincerely, his loyalty to Communism and to the Soviet Union.

To no avail.

Late at night on August 20, 1968 … two days after my second birthday … two thousand tanks and two hundred thousand soldiers poured across the Czech and Slovak borders.

Twenty-two years later, I would be standing on those cobblestones and discussing that event with people who experienced it firsthand; and I'd be obsessing about it in ways that are still hard for me to understand.

And *forty* years later I'd be writing about it. *Still* obsessed with an event that has absolutely nothing to do with me, my family, or my country. Why? If I could tell you that, I probably would have never written this book.

This book is, in part, my futile attempt to answer that question for myself.

III. Vivace con moto

I was paroled from Hodonín a couple of months before the fall semester started in Brno, so I found myself free again in Europe with lots of time to kill. I *didn't* have lots of money to burn, but I'll take time over money any day.

I decided to set out on a hitchhiking adventure to end all hitchhiking adventures, and to do it on a shoestring budget. This precluded lots of time in cities, since I'd need to pay for lodging if I did not want to get cozy with winos on the sidewalk.* No, I was going to see the countryside and set up my brand-new Czech tent wherever I happened to find myself at sunset, and live on bread and salami.

I told Jarka about my plan and she was a little concerned for me. So my first "ride" was with her family, heading west to the collective farm where her mother lived.

The countryside of southern Moravia really is beautiful. Yellow and green fields roll along and you hardly ever see a soul. Occasionally, you come across a granite statue of Mother Mary with a bent brass halo hanging crookedly off the back of her head. She still looks over these fields as she has for centuries, completely unperturbed by historical developments that we seem to find so important; nor by the fact that her halo isn't even on straight.

After thirty minutes or so driving through this blessed countryside, we pulled onto a gravel road leading up a hill, and surrounded by a sparse hardwood forest. We came to a dilapidated farmhouse with a concrete skimcoat over its wood framing, and pulled beside it. Attached to the house, and running behind it, was a split-fence enclosure which a variety of small animals called home. As we got

---

* Though winos, by the way, did not seem to exist in the East back then. "Parasites" were dealt with harshly in the Workers' Paradise.

out of the car I heard the aggressive *car cark* of a rooster and felt the wind rustle my hair. The pleasant aroma of fermenting oats mixed with that of distant manure, and my mind was transported back to the magical Berkshire Hills of my youth. I took in a deep breath of the stuff, and let it back out as slowly as I could manage.

Jarka's Mom was a widow, and a tough old *babuska*. Her hips were slightly wider than her broad shoulders, and she wore a green and blue dress of stiff sturdy fabric. Her blood-stained white apron seemed to be tied too tight, but seemed a permanent fixture nonetheless. I picture her sleeping dressed exactly as she was when I saw her standing there peeling potatoes over the sink.

The old lady wasn't mean to me, but made no effort to be a gracious hostess either. *"Yep, here you are. So?"*

Jarka tried hard to soften her mother's heart, and get her to accept me. *"Hey, Mom, this guy's our friend, and he's from America. Isn't that interesting?"* Not as interesting as peeling potatoes.

While Jarka helped her Mom prepare dinner, I went to set up my tent in the nearby woods. Since this was the first time I had done so, it took me all of twenty minutes. Soon I'd be an expert and slap that thing up anywhere anytime (even in the dark) in less than five.

Over dinner I couldn't help but notice that Jarka's mother ate … well … like a man. She shoveled food into her mouth in quick jerky motions. She spoke with her mouth full and curled her lips to keep that precious food from falling out. She hovered suspiciously over her plate as if to protect it from thieves. And all the while angry words spilled past the crushed food on her teeth.

My Czech was not good enough to understand the old *babuska*, so Jarka had to translate for me. She told me that her mother was griping about the recent amnesty.

A little background: the intellectual Václav Havel had spent many years in prison under the Communists for his "counter-revolutionary" writings. And the prison system in Czechoslovakia was, as they always are, a nasty affair. But this one even *more* troublesome because rapists and thieves were sometimes mixed in with priests and writers, and it was often hard to tell who was who and exactly why they were there. "President" Havel, trying to wade through this sticky problem in the first months of 1990, came up with a radical solution: let's free just about *everybody* and start from scratch. And that's exactly what he did. Eighteen years later it's still the most controversial thing he ever did, and the one he takes the most heat for.

So as you may understand, that evening, in the presence of an uninvited representative of the bourgeois West, the scandalous image of empty prison cells was burning bright in the mind of Jarka's Mom. And she was mighty pissed off. She snapped at me, "Under the Communists we never even had to lock our doors ... now I lock them all the time!"

After Jarka translated that sentence I gently asked the old lady, "Oh, have you had problems with criminals here?"

"Well, no."

"Then," I replied calmly, "it sounds to me like the only thing that has changed *here* since the Velvet Revolution is that you now lock your doors."

Jarka howled in laughter and it took her a solid minute before she could control herself well enough to tell her mother what I had just said.

I don't think I was scoring any new points with Comrade Babuska.

The next morning I said goodbye, stole an old copy of *Rudé Právo** from the old lady's garden shed, and hiked down the gravel road to start my journey.

---

* The Czech equivalent of Pravda: i.e. the official newspaper of the Czechoslovak Communist Party. I still have that stolen copy tucked into a bookcase and I sometimes wonder if I should return it to the old babuska. Of course I forget that I'm older now too, and that the old lady probably is no more.

My goal was to visit nearly all of the old remote castles in the Moravian and Bohemian countryside. There are many dozens of them from the Middle Ages and early Renaissance. There are perhaps even more baroque chateaus from 18th century, but I found those much less interesting.

These old castles were often built strategically in places that were hard to get to: like completely surrounded by water, or perched atop an impossibly steep hill. I guess there was a reason for that in those days before electronic security systems and 911.

Some of these places were virtually abandoned, and not guarded at all. At one, I deigned to imagine myself an invader and to test just how hard it would have been to breach the walls. I set my backpack down, and started climbing the rock hill — which was so steep that if I tried to sit I'm sure I would have started sliding and bouncing back down over sharp rocks. It was almost like cliff climbing, except that all of the holds were sharp black rocks of only forty pounds or so, none of which could be trusted. After climbing fifty feet or so (halfway to the fort's *true* wall) I saw something yellow sticking out from between two rocks. I grabbed it, and pulled it out. It was a bone. About one inch thick, with a joint on one end and a jagged broken edge four inches below that.*

I looked at the climb still ahead, and the twenty-foot sheer wall above that. I then looked at the broken fleshless bone in my hand. And said, "You know Mark, I think this would be a good time to head back down." So I did.

In southern Bohemia a powerful green Ford pulled over for me. With a car like that, I should have thought to address the driver in

---

* I have no idea who or what that bone came from, but I do still have it in my basement. I'd have its DNA tested but that would take the fun out of everything.

German, but that didn't occur to me for some reason. *"Dobrý den, děkuji!"* I said in my best (i.e. very poor) Czech. "Hey, man, you're American!" was the incredulous reply I got back.

It turned out this guy was one of a growing contingent of Czech ex-pats who had returned to spend the summer in their ancestral homeland. Throughout that summer of 1990 thousands of these guys showed up in droves.

This one was a little different though: he was younger. Maybe thirty or so. Most of the others I met had left just after the Russians came back to town in 1968, and they were twenty or thirty at that time. So in their forties and fifties when I met them.

One of these guys had escaped to The West in the most creative way — strapped to a hang-glider. He had left his parents, his siblings, his best friend, his lovers past and present, and everything he had ever known with nothing but an aluminum frame and some nylon sheets tied to his back. He just silently glided out of their lives forever. How the hell do you do that?! Had he really thought this through? Or was this just a youthful stunt? Maybe he had just broken up with a girlfriend and said in a moment of bitterness, "Ah, what the heck, I think I'll ride a thermal into Austria." Or maybe this was deeper. Maybe he really *did* feel that freedom was more important than anything else in the world. Maybe he did this stunt with his eyes wide open and a sharp knife stuck in his heart.

None of these questions really matter though. Because no matter *why* he left, or how he felt about it at the time, the fact is there was no going back. His soul could never be the same.

I ached for this guy. He came back two decades later to a land he could no longer call home. And to once-loved ones who had long ago given him up for dead, and did not care about him anymore. Nobody thought 1989 would ever happen, so hearts behaved accordingly: They mourned for a year or so and then moved on. Complicating things further is the fact the Communists made his family suffer for their blood-ties to a "traitor," and his scholarly big brother … the brother he loved … was forced into manual labor and prohibited from using that impressive brain of his for anything more than crossword puzzles.

Our adolescent hang-glider tried to re-connect with ex-family and ex-friends, but nobody could understand the man he had become; and worse, they didn't care. His much-aged brother tried not to hold him responsible for two decades of sewer-line repair, but couldn't quite manage. He was an unwelcome stranger now — even in his mother's eyes.

His story is not unusual at all – thousands of guys experienced exactly the same thing in the summer of 1990. They knew it would be this way even before they came back, but they knew they had to try. Some are *still* trying. But most went back to their lives and their wives in the suburbs of Sydney or Toulouse or Cleveland; and tried once again to forget about the past.

Sorry, I got sidetracked again: I was talking about a ride in a green Ford. The driver said he had been an orphan in Prague, and somehow ended up being adopted in America as an eight-year-old boy. I know, it sounds somewhat implausible — as did many of the things he told me. The facts are that he spoke perfect English with a subtle midwestern accent and that he was very proficient in Czech. The rest I can't be so sure of.

He took me to a roadside diner of sorts in a small Czech village, and said he would treat me to lunch. Man lives not by bread and salami alone, so this sounded good to me. *Maybe some soup or something?*

He chatted with the waitress, who was a plain-looking brunette of about twenty. She never smiled, but just wrote on her pad and spoke in monotone replies. She *did* speak more than one would if simply taking an order, but I have no idea what she was saying or what the two of them were talking about other than food. It was all Czech to me.

After she left our table to place our order my new traveling companion said, "You probably didn't notice, but she's beautiful. She tries to hide that because she's a very sensitive girl. She always cries right after we fuck."

When our waitress brought our food I looked again and tried to see her from this guy's erotically charged perspective, but I couldn't pull it off. She still looked like a bland provincial waitress to me.

My new buddy called himself Mike. He was a bit on the short side, with a stocky muscular build that had a hint of pudginess to it. His skin had a subtle and unusual green sheen. He spoke quickly and while doing so often jerked his head back and forth almost imperceptibly.

He told me that he was staying in a cabin at a local campground, and invited me to spend the night there instead of setting up in the woods. I had been trying to spend one night per week in a place with a shower, so this sounded even better than the soup I had just enjoyed. I *was* very overdue. I had just swum and rinsed my clothes in the river winding around one of those remote castles, but that's not the same. And the water did have a green algae tint that I didn't quite trust.

The cabin at the campground was pretty big. It was the sort of place you recall from summer camp: a large sturdy shack with no heat and no plumbing and bunkbeds all around. It could have slept eight easily, but Mike had it all to himself. He was living large on his American dollars.

Mike told me about his job in the psychology department of a mid-western university, and about a girlfriend who lived just north of Prague. He then quickly pulled out a Polaroid picture of her as if to prove he wasn't making anything up. The pale girl was naked, lying on a hill in the sunshine. Normally in this situation, one guy is supposed to say to another, "Oh, she's very pretty!" But I couldn't say that, because I couldn't know. All I can tell you about her is that her pubic hair was auburn, since the composition ran from just above her navel to just below her knees. I don't remember what I *did* say, I just (as usual) remember what I was thinking: *"Man, why the hell did you just show me that?"*

I slept great on that campground mattress. Still in my sleeping bag of course, but now with no sticks or rocks underneath me. "Ah, luxury!" But the next day, I started to feel a little off. My perceptions were cloudy, even though the sun blazed brightly: I was coming down with a fever.

Mike graciously suggested I stay in the cabin with him until I got better, which I gratefully did. I stayed on that cozy mattress for twenty hours per day four days straight. I didn't sleep more than twelve hours per day, but spent another eight paralyzed in bed, staring at the empty bunk above me and thinking. Unless Mike was there, when I would stare at the empty bunk above me and listen to his half-truths as he fired them at me for hours on end.

Mike left every day to do God-knows-whom, and one afternoon while he was gone I found myself laying there and thinking about love, marriage, and fate. I thought about Hope, the Long Island Catholic girl who had no idea what she meant to me.

I got out of my bed, and sat down to write a letter: I had to let her know. To at least give it a shot without passively allowing my life to move on without her.

When I was just about done with my bizarre love note, Mike came back. He saw me stuff my paper into a book and asked, "Whattaya workin' on?"

"Oh, I was just writing to a university back in the States."

"What?!" Mike barked. *"Are you checking up on me?!!"* Then he carefully studied my face, looking for clues.

"Uh ... actually ... no. No Mike, I wasn't doing that at all. It was just about some girl. A girl, I ..."

My red-faced bunkmate still looked pretty angry, so I decided that I felt well enough to hit the road again. Next stop, Pilsen.

I got picked up by a really nice couple of Czechs in their mid-thirties who lived in Pilsen. We spoke a mish-mash of Czech, German, and English and got by with it just fine. It was clear they were extremely pleased to have pulled over for me, only to discover to their shock and delight that I was American. I was like a little trophy they had been awarded for their kindness toward hitchhikers.

They were on their way back home and invited me to stay with them. "Well, I did already have a shower this morning. But why not?!"

They took a detour for my sake to the wife's hometown, Klatovy, and there they coldly pointed out in the main square a bronze plaque honoring the Soviet Army for liberating Czechoslovakia in World War Two. Bursting out from this plaque was a relief statue of a Soviet soldier carrying an adoring four-year-old Czech girl in one arm, and a bouquet of flowers in the other.

But then they excitedly showed me a brighter plaque that had just been remounted after spending forty years in cold storage. It featured the emblem of Czechoslovakia beside another emblem with a Bald Eagle on it. The eagle clasped an olive branch in one set of talons, and a half-dozen sharp arrows in the other. Beneath that emblem, in English, these words:

> TO
> FUTURE GENERATIONS
> IN REMEMBRANCE
> OF THE LIBERATION
> OF KLATOVY
> ON 5TH MAY 1945
> FROM THE GERMAN
> OPPRESSORS
> BY GENERAL G.S.

PATTON'S THIRD
U.S. ARMY.
THIS PLAQUE
IS PRESENTED
BY THE TOWN
OF KLATOVY

As we continued onto Pilsen they told me stories that, though I'd been a history buff for three whole years, I had never heard before. About how Patton and his men liberated this region and then had to sit there doing nothing on strict orders from Eisenhower; since Roosevelt had already promised Prague to Stalin. FDR would not, under any circumstance, go back on his word and beat Uncle Joe to that glorious prize on the Vltava.

Patton was furious, and while his men drank beer and enjoyed the favors of Czech beauties he kept calling Ike and complaining, "What the fuck, Sir, I had the Krauts on the run! Now we're just *sitting here* while the Reds are on the move!" Patton hated the Communists with a passion; and saw this two-front war as a race to determine the future of Europe: free, or slave. That's a view you're unlikely to hear from an American history professor, but it was accepted as a tautology by these humble Czechs. Patton's name conjures yet another "what if" in the history of the Czech nation, and he's still a hero with the common folk in Pilsen.*

You know the song, *Roll Out the Barrel?* That's a Czech pop tune from the '30's that American soldiers learned during their vacation in Pilsen: Another little tid-bit I picked up during my 24-hours there. I got to hear it sung both in Czech and in heavily accented English. *"Role aut da badel!"* A drinking song never sounded so beautiful.

I'm sure I could have stayed with this kind couple indefinitely, but I resolved to make it a pleasant one-night-stand and keep moving.

---

* Or I should say Patton was still a hero in 1990. Now that Dukes of Hazard re-runs have been dubbed into Czech, I wonder if he may be forgotten.

I still had a lot of ground to cover, and had to make up for lost time in that Boy Scout cabin.

I headed back south, where there were a few more castles on my list, then west toward the West German border. Many of the towns I was seeing here had been predominantly German before the War; now they were 100% Czech. They seemed slightly under-populated, and many of them seemed to have a dark, lifeless cloud hanging over them. More than a few people lived there bodily, but fewer in spirit.

I got a ride across the border into West Germany, which was a first for me ... I was used to passing customs on foot, not in the comfort of a stranger's car. These people took me all the way through the *Bayerischer Walt*, but once we got to the Autobahn they needed to head south whereas I needed to go north. So they left me beside the onramp heading toward Bayreuth, my destination.

I had at this point been living on the road for three weeks, and other than my few days with a fever everything had gone wonderfully. I had been hiking down country roads and turning to stick out a thumb anytime I heard a car approaching. I hiked a lot, but not because people wouldn't stop. It was just that so few cars passed down those remote roads. I don't think I was ever passed up by more than five cars before one pulled over to offer me a ride. Whether on foot or in someone's car, I had truly been enjoying myself.

Here in Germany, that was about to change. You can't exactly stroll down the Autobahn with a backpack on sticking out a thumb beside you. Standing in place next to that onramp was my only option, and it wasn't much fun. Hundreds of cars accelerated hard beside me, their drivers oblivious to my pleading eyes. Humble Volkswagens pushed their little engines for all they were worth, and roaring Porsches did the same.

The smell of all this exhaust probably turned me green, and made me look even less appealing to kind hearts … if such things beat around there at all. Around the sixth hour I started looking around to figure out where I might set up a tent. It wasn't a very hospitable area for that. Around the eighth hour, just when I was wondering how I could get myself back to Czechoslovakia, a big silver BMW pulled over. I hesitated for a millisecond … "wait, what's the catch?" But then quickly threw my backpack in the backseat, jumped in the front, and said *"Danke shön!"*

"No problem, where ya headed," the driver replied in perfect American television English. He was a white-haired German of about forty-five. A little too young to have lost all the color in his hair, but just about the right age to be driving a new top-of-the-line Beemer.

When I said "Bayreuth" I learned to my delight that's where he was headed too … to visit his mother. *"Thank God I don't have to hitchhike again today!"*

As we zoomed smoothly down the highway an alarm binged and a warning light flashed on his dashboard. He seemed unfazed but I had to ask, "What was that?"

"Oh, the car is new and I'm not supposed to take it over 160." (i.e. 100MPH)

It seemed to me very un-German of him to ignore such clear instructions, but that's exactly what he did. I guess he really loved his Mom.

In Bayreuth, I had an acquaintance expecting me – a German kid a couple of years younger than me who had invited me to spend a few days with his family. I cannot remember his name; even more disturbing, I cannot remember how, where, or when we met. That depresses me.

Bayreuth is famous (some would say notorious) because Wagner lived and worked here, and Wagner lovers from all over the world now descend here every summer to lose themselves in his Ring Cycle. The notorious part comes from the fact that Hitler too was a Wagner nut, and showered his affections (with the Reich's stolen loot) on this humble little town.

The locals just call it home, and pretend that Wagner means nothing to them. Please don't even mention Hitler, that's getting very old by now.

My nameless friend still lived with his mother in a fairly large house on the outskirts of the city, next to a sweeping field. I never saw his Dad, and I don't know what the deal was there.

As chance would have it, when I stopped by another visitor showed up … my friend's much older brother. He had just rented a Cessna and flown himself down from Frankfurt, since he happened to be in Germany on business. He lived, I learned, in the Philippines. With the mail-order bride he had bought after striking it rich.

It seems this guy had an innate knack for earning the confidence of third-world generalissimos and connecting them with first-world weaponry. *"I ahm an ahms deelah!"* he told me loudly with his eyes wide open and whites exposed around the full periphery of his transparent blue irises.

I didn't know if I should tell him that I was quite pleased with my new *St. Etienne* .22 or if I should just keep my mouth shut. I opted for the latter. He probably didn't think much of Gallic weaponry anyway.

I think it was hard on my friend's Mom to simultaneously play hostess to a foreign stranger and an ex-pat son. I tried to stay out of her hair as much as possible, and spent my time either drinking beer with her youngest son or wandering around Bayreuth trying to figure out what this place was all about and why it somehow reminded me of Joseph Conrad.

I hung out with my new friend and his friends for several days. They were pretty ordinary middle-class kids who absorbed kitschy rock tunes and Beethoven with equal indifference. I remember sitting with them in my friend's bedroom once and one of them said,

"Hey Mark, check this out … the dog loves Beethoven!" They put on a CD of one of the late quartets and sure enough, the dog got up, sat down next to the speaker, and tilted his head just like the RCA dog. Pretty cool trick.

Later, as we sat lounging around with nothing to do, my friend's best friend felt compelled to talk about the 1930's and (without mentioning anything or anyone by name) the rise of Hitler. He said with an unusual air of seriousness, as if he needed to explain something very important to me, "Germany wants never again to be isolated from the international community." I can only guess that was the official explanation in public schools, because this kid did not strike me as much of a thinker. Somebody else does his thinking for him, and we should watch *that* person very closely. These kids would just as readily accept different lessons.

One afternoon, when I was wandering around Bayreuth, I found myself in front of a concert hall. I seem magnetically attracted to those. There was a poster advertising a concert of chamber music to be held that evening: Brahms, Beethoven, and one lesser composer were on the program. I bought a ticket. Just one, since I did not know if my friend would want to go. And I did not really want a male date anyway.

I would later find out that this place I had accidentally found was "Margrave's Opera House," considered by architecture buffs one of the most extraordinary baroque theaters in the world. Wagner conducted here before building the now much more famous *Festspielhaus*.

My recollection of the Margrave is that it was very small and intimate. I cannot imagine a Wagner work being staged there… it's nowhere near big enough for all that noise and all that action! Perhaps the stage is big enough, I don't remember that. I just remember the seating, and how close the two sides of the auditorium were to each other. Rows of seats were stacked on top of each other three stories high, and I sat in a front-row seat mid-point in the theater facing not the stage, but the identical three-story stack of seats in front of me. I remember being lost in thought listening to Brahms and then having the creepy feeling that somebody was watching me. I remember looking across the theatre to a seat not forty feet from me, where a pretty girl of about my age sat staring at me with a subtle grin. She was attractive enough, so I was willing to play her game: I stared back at her and tried to imitate that wry grin. But after a minute of this visual intercourse I determined that there was really nothing behind that pretty face that interested me, and I grew fatigued. (For some reason German girls could never keep my attention for long – not even the rare pretty ones.) I broke off our staring contest, accepted defeat, and crooked my neck to look at the performers on stage.

I tried to fall again into the rapture of Brahms, but could not do so. I still felt those demanding eyes burning on my ears, and I found my mind transported back to Milan, 1987. What is it about opera houses and itinerant journeys? Or is it something about me?

Back then I was between semesters at the University of Rouen, and blazing through Europe on another month-long Euro-rail pass. In Milan I found myself (yes, almost accidentally) in front of *La Scala* just an hour before Wagner's *Flying Dutchman* was scheduled to go on. Isn't that ironic? Here I am in Wagner's adopted hometown being ogled by the aggressive granddaughter of a Nazi and remembering the first time I ever heard Wagner performed. The parallels get even stranger, but I'll get to that in a minute.

In Milan for one night of a whirlwind Euro-rail tour, and indifferent to the fact that I was wearing completely faded jeans with holes in the knees, I bought a ticket to see "a show" in the stuffiest old opera house in the world. I knew virtually nothing about Wagner at that time, and certainly did not know the story or the music to this particular opera. I did not know any of the famous names on the program, and really had no idea more generally what I had gotten myself into.

I waited in line behind a man in a tuxedo so I could check my dusty backpack in the lobby. That done, I strode into the hall and wound my way through a sea of middle-aged women dripping with diamonds and caked with pasty makeup. I found my way to my seat and sat; truly oblivious to the outrageous, scandalous thing I had just done.

The music did not move me at all, but I did concentrate fully on the stage and the strange sounds charging out of the pit — trying hard to make sense of it all. And then, I had that funny feeling. I looked away from the stage to a seat about forty feet to my right, where a tall thin man of about thity-five sat staring at me with a Cheshire-cat grin. I gave him a polite nod and quickly looked back toward the stage. I kept my eyes on the stage but my mind stayed focused on the periphery of my vision, where I could see those hungry eyes trying to eat me from a distance. *"Oh, going to the opera is not nearly as much fun as I imagined."*

During intermission, this bird of prey swooped down on me and said, "You're an American, aren't you? Well so am I!"

He then informed me quickly that he was an architect from New York, and that he was gay. *"Wow, what are the odds?! I'm a student from Connecticut and I'm straight. Can we stop talking now?"*

Thankfully, the parallels stop there: that aggressive *fraulein* in the Margrave did not swoop down on me during intermission — I guess she was traditional enough to know that was my role.

And if you don't know a good thing when you see one staring you in the face that's your problem asshole so why don't you just go back to your crummy new world and eat a Hamburger or something — that's a German word you know and Frankfurter is too but you don't even know that so aufweidersehen im hölle you loser.

One day, brother arms dealer took us all for a ride in the Cessna. Private aviation has been a huge deal in this part of Germany since … oh, since 1933 or so. I had never seen so many small planes and gliders in my life.

Our pilot talked a little bit less than was his wont while flying, but still did make frequent loud statements in his harsh German. When he spoke, his eyes always lit up like they were on fire. When he was quiet, they cooled down instantly and became glazed.

Throughout the flight Mom had a half-smile which clearly displayed her mixed emotions. For the most part, enjoying herself and proud of her wealthy son. But the joy did not go very deep. Her better interior self had long ago set up a barrier to disconnect itself from the surface.

We were at an altitude that surely allowed us to see into Czechoslovakia, not all that far away really. I commented on that. Or maybe I asked, "Is that Czechoslovakia over there?" Mom suddenly lost what was left of her smile and all six eyes near me glazed over.

Somebody finally broke the silence with some nonsensical comment, just to be polite: I had obviously raised a sore subject. *"What, that there are no longer any Germans on the other side of that frontier? That there is a frontier at all? That what was once part of Das Reich is now something else? That filthy Slavs live so close that you can almost see them from the air? That filthy Slavs live?"*

Or maybe it was just that living so close to the front line of the Cold War for so long had taken its toll on their psyches, and they preferred to forget what was over there.

I'll never know exactly what was going through their minds at that moment, I only know that I suddenly felt anxious to get back on the ground, and to get back on the other side of The Curtain. To get back home.

I luckily got a ride to the border quite easily, and once again walked through customs. I explored a few uninteresting towns, and spent one night in a remote wood. Then hitched a ride to my next destination.

Karlovy Vary is a strange new name (to most ears) for a town better known to historians as *Karlsbad*. This marble spa resort, with its natural hot springs, has a storied history. Goethe and Beethoven once walked its streets together discussing, I'm sure, "the fine weather we are having," and "the benefits of mineral salts." This town was once predominantly German-speaking, and a prized jewel of the *Sudetenland* that France and Britain, in their shortsighted cowardice, gave to Hitler *gratis* in 1938.

In my bookshelf I have a black hardbound copy of *College German*, my grandfather's textbook from 1939. It is a marvelous historical document in so many ways: the old German Script, the antiquated literary language, and the two-page map of the *Deutches Reich* under its hardbound covers. On that map most of Europe is white, but a menacing blob is shaded gray ... a snapshot of the growing *Reich*. Karlsbad was within that dark blob, but *Prag* was not – yet. Just months after that textbook went to press the blob had nearly doubled in size, and included *all* of my beloved Czech lands. So *this* was the Germany my grandfather saw as he learned German so he could read Freud and Marx in the original. (Maybe Luther too?)

I often think about the *Sudentenland* from many different perspectives. One, the perspective of a Czech man in 1938 whose honor had been simultaneously spat upon by the callous and the cowardly. Another, from the perspective of a German-speaking schoolgirl a decade later, who had been marched out of the only home she'd ever known because her town was suddenly decreed

100% Czech. I think of that German girl's tearful farewell to her Czech neighbor, whom she had the naivety to befriend during the war. I think about the Czech family who moved into the house after it had been stolen from that little girl's parents. Who decided these particular Czechs could live there? Why them and not another? What right did they have to be there? Did they feel even a little guilty about taking over a stranger's home? Or was it "just desserts for the Germans?" But were not the German families really being expelled, in a way, because the French and British had let the Czechs down in 1938? Would the German expulsion have ever happened without Munich? Whose fault *was* this really? Hitler's of course, but he's dead. Who else should we blame?

I think about it too in broader philosophical terms: is collective punishment of a nation ever justified? Are we not individuals with individual souls and individual responsibilities? As with most big questions, I find no simple answers.

After a couple of pleasant but lonely days in that spa resort, I hitched my way though the mountains along the Czech/East German border, to a place not far from Poland. I had heard tales about this region: treeless moonscapes murdered by pollution. I wanted to see it for myself. It wasn't as bad as people had told me, but I do still recall it as one of the most depressing places on earth. Almost nobody lives there, and I'm very fortunate I managed to get rides and not find myself marooned.

I headed north across the border into what was then still called East Germany. There was no official plan for reunification yet, but everyone knew that there would be one soon. It was clear that before long the *DDR* would be no more, and I was almost desperate to get those three letters stamped in my passport. So I casually asked the drab green official to stamp my passport. But he just as casually refused. I then pleaded, *"Oh, bitte shön!"*

"Nein!" He knew exactly what I was up to and he wanted no part of it. He pushed the closed passport into my chest with one hand and gave me a backhanded wave with the other. *"Geh."*

I got a ride to Dresden I guess, though I can't remember that leg at all. I do remember pulling into a city straight out of my history books. It looked almost exactly like the pictures from 1946 I had seen. Still a bombed-out mess. Oh, I suppose 90% of it had been rebuilt, but the 10% still left in ruins was the only part I could see. It was hard to remember that I had not even been born when those firebombs fell.

There was something very wrong with the people there. I couldn't quite put my finger on it, but somehow Auden's Post-War poetry still rang true in that ruinous spectacle: A barren cityscape populated by *homo sapiens,* but not by human beings:

That girls are raped, that two boys knife a third,
Were axioms to him, who had never heard
Of any world where promises are kept,
Or one could weep because another wept.

W.H. Auden: <u>The Shield of Achilles</u>

Virgil mercifully led me out of that inferno, and I headed northwest toward Wittenberg. I had to see where Hamlet, the hero of my imagination, had gone to college.

During this sixty-day hitchhiking tour, I became an expert in Communist cars. I quickly came to understand that the Czech-made *Škodas* were by far the best of the bunch. I'm not saying this because of my irrational attachment to the Czechs, it's just an incontrovertible truth. All of the other East-bloc cars were poorly designed, poorly manufactured, and prone to fall apart at any moment. That even goes for the Russian-made *Volga*, which was a big powerful car made for the Communist elite. Yes, it was big. Yes, it was powerful. Yes, it said loud and clear, "Move over, the most equal animal of all needs to get through!!" But below its heavy surface, it was just another breakdown waiting to happen. A big honking piece of crap.

But the humble *Škoda* just kept going and going. I don't mean to imply they were the best cars in the world – far from it. I think their quality and reliability was probably similar to that of a Volkswagen from the '70's. Which is to say head-and-shoulders above anything else produced in the East.

The lowest man on this vehicular totem pole was the East German *Trabant* – affectionately nick-named *"Trabby."* This "car" was an unmitigated disaster so complete that it was hilarious, and everybody loved it for that reason. It was like the drunk uncle who always makes weddings so much interesting. You're embarrassed to be seen with him, but you can't help yourself. He's fun.

The runner up for the honors of worst car in the world was the other East German: the *Wartburg*. This was a little bigger than the lovable Trabby, which made it more comfortable but less adorable. Like the Trabby, it had a two-stroke engine. You know, the kind that burns oil on purpose and smokes a lot? Like a chainsaw? Yeah, one of those. I rode to Wittenberg in a luxurious *Wartburg*.

In my mind Wittenberg was simply the old college town that Gertrude had famously asked Hamlet not to go back to. But considering the fact that "Hamlet" was never in Wittenberg in the first place — nor in Denmark for that matter — historians are probably more likely to tell you that Luther nailed his 95 theses to a wooden door here in 1517.

While looking for Hamlet in all the wrong places, I ran into an American professor. I don't mean a professor I already knew, just an American who happened to be a professor. At that point Americans were still a relatively rare sight in this part of Germany, and stuck out like dandelions in a landfill. We pegged each other immediately as compatriots and struck up a conversation in English.

The guy had some old family roots in this area, and maybe that's why he felt compelled to enjoy his sausage the way he did … proud to allow its molten fat to dribble down his chin for several seconds before nostalgically dabbing it with a grease-stained napkin.

As we stood there talking in the square, a faded orange Wartburg rattled past us blowing dark black smoke out of its long skinny tailpipe. *"RAT-a-tat-tat-tat-RAT-a-tat-tat-tat."*

I commented jokingly about the irony that while Germans working in a free market economy produced Mercedes, BMW, and Porsche, this Wartburg was the best idea the Germans could come up with under Communism. Professor Sausage did not appreciate my observation at all, and explained with great erudition that the Rhineland and Bavaria had *always* been more industrialized than Saxony.

"Oh, so *that's* why Western cars are so much better!" I was having another one of those experiences where I had to quietly observe a smart person saying something really stupid, and keep my inner dialogue to myself.

I don't think my comparison of East vs. West German cars is all that interesting, since the conclusions are pretty obvious. But I think one subject *is* worth looking into, and that's this: of all the East Bloc cars, doesn't it seem odd that the undisputed worst ones came from *Germany?* I mean, even the Romanian *Dacias* were better than these! Why? I don't have a good answer to this, which is of course why I find it an interesting question.

That sausage-stained professor, that smelly Wartburg, and Luther's famous church are, I'm afraid, the only things I remember about Wittenberg. Next stop, Berlin.

Berlin is a truly frightening place. Set on a flat plain where you can see forever, you look and look and all you can see in the distance is … Berlin. It's huge.

The Wall had been breached nine months prior, but vast stretches of it still remained perfectly intact — even though every day thousands of people beat on it with sledgehammers and tie rods. I was one of those thousands. The Wall was so big, and so long, that it could take a very prolonged brutal beating and still be there.

There was still a sense of newness and excitement in the air; and you could still easily pick out of the crowd a pale skinny East German in drab clothing and worn-out shoes as he wandered aimlessly around West Berlin clutching a precious banana in his hands.

Young people from all over the world were having a summer-long party in Berlin, which seemed a little grotesque to me when I thought of that guy and his banana. Everyone was proud to be "a part of history" just because they beat on a wall and filled their pockets with concrete crumbs. They got drunk and staggered across no-man's land pretending that it was an accomplishment not to get shot. In the first months of 1989 two guys *did* get shot here (if only they had waited!) and their blood puddled on the same soil which now found itself stained with Australian vomit.

I felt a little guilty as I stabbed that wall with the end of a tie-rod, but I had to do it. *Veni, vidi.* I couldn't leave out the *vici* even though I wanted to, and even though I felt like a pathetic poseur. All the world's a stage, and that was my part to play that day.

On the streets of East Berlin, I saw a black-and-white postcard for sale. It had two pictures on it: one, the broken Wall near Brandenburg Gate. Two, the official portrait of East Germany's president Erich Honecker. Running below both pictures were these words: *"Die Mauer wird in 1000 Jahren noch bleiben."* ("The Wall will still be standing 1000 years from now.")

This was an intentional misquote — Honecker had in fact said "50-100 years." He said that in January 1989, and The Wall came down ten months later.

This was also a cruel joke with historical undertones. The Germans have long had some bizarre mystical attachment to the idea of millennia, and Hitler had plugged into this directly when he spoke of a "Reich that would last a thousand years." This was not true of course, but poetic dreams do find fertile root in the mystical German heart. The siren calls of pagan mysticism have caused the German nation great pain over the years. Would it were they were the only nation that suffered.

I stayed in Berlin for several days witnessing, but not participating in, that drunken party. I had been on the road for about a month now, living close to the locals. In Berlin I suddenly found myself surrounded by Americans, Australians, and Brits; and found myself forced to be one of them. But I didn't *want* to be one of them! They were obnoxious brats who didn't give a shit about anything outside themselves, and who had an inflated sense of their own importance in the grand scheme of things. "History" for them was just an egocentric exercise about bragging rights. I imagine these kids would have arrived at Auschwitz a few months after the last rotten corpse had been pulled out of there, then tapped a keg and dubbed themselves liberators. "Yeah, *fryheight* man — let the party begin!" They all made me nauseous, and I had to get out of there.

I made myself yet another cardboard sign, "Leipzig," and got myself to the outskirts of the city. Before long, I found myself in the front seat of a blue Trabby, and in the company of an East German guy of about my age. Burning oil had never smelled so good.

Once again I found myself invited to spend the night in a humble cramped apartment, and once again I accepted gratefully.

Leipzig is a wonderful little city (at least in its old center) and neither Allied bombs nor Communist ideology were able to destroy that beauty completely. It has been a prominent center of commerce since the twelfth century, and that tradition continued even under Communism, since Comecon members from other East Bloc countries sometimes met there to barter goods and services.

The University of Leipzig opened in 1409, and soon thereafter Leipzig became known as the publishing capital of Germany. The love of books still permeates the air there, and strangely the Communists did not manage to change that either.

Once upon a time, Goethe called Leipzig "a little Paris". That was back when the word "Paris" was synonymous with classical learning and The Sorbonne: i.e. a long time ago.

Leipzig's second-greatest claim to fame is another ideologically dangerous one: its association with Bach and his religious music. Bach lived and worked there from 1723-1750 and composed many of his greatest works for the small audience of Leipzig's *Thomaskirche.*

"Ah, Bach and books … I think I can stay here for a while!" I did — for two weeks to be exact. I was welcome to stay as long as I cared to, provided I pitched in for the food budget. There was virtually nothing in the grocery stores but pasta and tomato paste, so that was a pretty simple requirement.

My new friend's apartment was tiny, dilapidated, and inhabited by three young men. With me, make that four. I slept in my sleeping bag on the floor. Though humble and cramped, I found it glorious since it was only a short walk from the *Thomaskirche,* where I was able to hear Bach's Preludes performed on what I imagined to be the same organ Bach had performed them on himself.

I later learned that was not the case: Bach's organ does not exist anymore. But please don't bother me with facts too much.

SOLI DEO GLORIA

Birds softly drowned
by sharp but slow staccato
mind not, perhaps enjoy
the man who took this motto.

BACH

Human Math
Natural at least
and discovered
not created.

Well, once
but not now or then
and always.

I spent at least half of every day in the *Deutsches Bücherei*, one of the largest and most famous libraries in the world. There I read books on Bach, Luther, and Goethe – trying to make sense of the latter two (I'm still not quite there) and reading up on the former just for fun. I also read about God and Man and how these two essences relate to one another.

I was shocked to see the incredible amount of serious Christian theology one could find on these shelves. Had the authorities not noticed? Didn't they care? I guess it was naïve of me to see this stuff as a threat to the regime, but that's how I felt at the time.

Leipzig, besides being an attractive medium-sized city, has one other thing in common with Pilsen: it too was captured by American troops and then later ceded to the Russians. Though of course there would be no memorial *here* to that fact; and there was no latent groundswell of gratitude toward Americans unfolding amongst the common *volk* in 1990.

My roommates for those weeks were, I assume, students at the university. Though they seemed just a few years too old for that. It occurs to me now, for the first time, that I have no idea what they were up to really. It was summer, so maybe they were between semesters. Maybe grad students? They did introduce me to quite a few other people of about my age, and we often sat in the café near the old town hall and talked politics.

I was fascinated, though not really angered, to hear these educated twenty-somethings defend Communism. Which they did almost universally and unapologetically. I had met young people from all over the East Bloc: Ukraine, Poland, Czechoslovakia, Hungary, Romania, etc. Never once had I heard a young person from those countries say anything nice about Communism. But here in East Germany, the red star still seemed hip after more than forty years of poverty and persecution: "Communism was a good idea that we didn't get quite right." Wow.

These kids were a little uncertain about the future, but for the most part were excited about the prospects of German re-unification. Because it could mean a fresh start and another go at Communism: this time with all of Germany instead of an isolated sliver. This time, they'd get it right.

Speaking with these young people, and living with them, gave me insights into the post-Christian German mind deeper than any I had previously experienced. It's a frighteningly bizarre place, where truth has no meaning outside the context of ideology. Where gullibility takes on a brand new, terrible, and strangely intelligent dimension. Where convictions feel completely unbothered by contradictory realities. Where totalitarianism has innate emotional appeal. Where "freedom" means anything but what that word normally connotes. Where language itself is a prisoner in a labyrinth with no exits.

Why are these Europeans so un-European? Could they be fundamentally flawed because the Romans never conquered and civilized their ancestors? Or is that historical fact just evidence of *another* fact that goes back even further? Is it evil of me to ask these questions about "a nation?" Since, as I'm the first to insist, every human being is an individual with an individual soul?

For a fairly brief period of history, the spirit and example of Christ ruled in the German lands and made these intelligent people some of the most civilized the world had ever known. Yet beneath that polished veneer lay the untamed brutishness of a wolf that had hidden in the woods: secretly laughing at Rome's domesticated, emasculated dogs. Once German philosophers peeled off the veneer of Christianity and extolled newly named virtues beneath, it didn't take long for the proud wolf to start hunting boldly in the open fields of Europe.

Personally, I am glad that so many of today's Germans are fond of David Hasselhoff and TV game shows. I'm glad that they think that the deepest spiritual value is self-esteem, and that the twin pillars of successful living are getting and spending. I'm glad they never leave room in their lives for thoughts about mortality — or about much of anything for that matter. I'm glad that they are so much like Americans: addicted to the cheap ideas, emotions, and stuff that television sells them. I pray that the Germans stay contented with their shallow successes, just like we do. Because if misfortune ever visits Germany again, Europe will be in trouble. One man there will start to think, and start to speak. And he'll find one hundred million credulous ears aching to hear.

This is all very unkind, and it especially pains me to write these words when I recall some individual Germans of whom I am very fond. I often hate myself for my opinions, but I will not lie about them and hate myself even more for my dishonesty. My honest opinion is this: While vapid culture and numbing materialism keep America from becoming her best, they keep Germany from becoming her worst.

Please, Germany, the next time you have triple-digit inflation and massive unemployment; the next time you are cold and hungry; the next time you feel like nobody in the world understands you, please, prove me wrong. I love to be wrong sometimes.

Sadly resigned to my new prejudices (ones I had vocally resisted for years), yet oddly with a deepened love for German books and music, I headed south … back toward my homeland.

IV. ANDANTE CANTABILE

BEFORE I had begun my summer-long adventure, I had already found an apartment in Brno thanks to one of my students in Hodonín. She knew a twenty-two-year-old kid lucky enough to suddenly find himself in sole possession of the luxurious apartment he had grown up in: a three-room flat of about eight hundred square feet on "Russian Street" in Královo Pole, an upper-middle-class neighborhood built between the wars. Many street names in Brno have changed since 1989, but *Ruská* still bears that questionable name today— because it was so named long *before* that country became associated with tanks and puppets. It runs off of "Slavonic Square," as do *Srbská, Slovenská, Charvatská,* and *Bulharská.* My crammed suitcase spent the summer of 1990 there on Russian Street, and in early September I showed up with the balance of my possessions strapped to my back.

My muscles bulged as I effortlessly dismounted the heavy pack and slowly lowered it to the floor. Though I had ingested a typically vitamin-deficient and inadequate East Bloc diet for months, I was in better shape than I had ever been when I had all the riches of America at my disposal.

My new roommate was called *František* by his mother, and *Franta* by his friends. To me, he became "Frank." Frank was tall with a medium unathletic build, pale skin prone to perspiration and pimples, and a shy smile that just made you love him. Though nearly a decade past puberty, he had still not outgrown adolescent awkwardness; and that painfully evident fact endeared him to everyone he met.

Frank gave me the best of the three rooms in the place: the room his parents used to call theirs, and the only one that could properly be called a bedroom. It was unusually spacious (probably 14'x12') and had large glass doors leading to a tiny balcony with a view of the backyard garden shared by the whole block. This garden took up at least an acre of real estate, and was surrounded by balconies like mine on all sides. My bedroom was furnished with a small work desk with a bookshelf above, a double bed for me to call my own (or to share as I saw fit), and a large modernistic armoire of brown laminate to amply contain my Spartan belongings. This pleasant little space would soon become the center of my universe.

Frank slept in an alcove hidden by a curtain and built into the wall of a 10'x10' room that was clearly *intended* to be a dining room, but which Frank had furnished with black faux-leather sofas, a square glass coffee table, and a modest stereo system. So there we ate a little awkwardly on soft sofas: with plates either balanced on our laps or placed uncomfortably low on a smoked-glass table.

The hidden alcove in the wall did not allow enough headroom for Frank to sit up in bed, but it was large enough to fit the queen-size mattress he slept on. Hence it was *also* large enough for him to have company ... though he never did. Above and below this alcove, the apartment's storage. It was all a remarkably efficient use of space akin to something one expects to see on a submarine or a spaceship.

Off the other side of this room ran a 4'x6' galley kitchen where, once a week, Frank would concoct with pride a spicy pot of Hungarian goulash. I can't remember what we cooked the rest of the week, but I do remember grinding a few tablespoons of coffee beans in our little kitchen every morning so Frank and I could enjoy a gritty cup of Turkish.

The 14'x14' living room, the largest of the troika, remained completely unfurnished and forgotten. Its dusty industrial carpet rarely felt anyone's feet, and we usually kept its translucent door closed to avoid looking into its depressing emptiness as we walked down the narrow hallway. This apartment had formerly housed a family of four, and with only two bachelors in it now at least *one* room would surely become superfluous.

Královo Pole was the ideal location for me: quiet, yet within walking distance of my new job at Masaryk University. In my ample free time I could effortlessly pick up a tram on either *Husitská* or

Hradecká and be in Brno's historic center or, with a few train changes, anywhere else in Europe. Once in a while I'd take a northbound tram or bus to the rural outskirts of the city. There I would hike on forgotten trails through hilly forests and spook herds of tiny roe deer. Occasionally I'd spot a muscular ram standing boldly on a ridgetop and staring at me like the intruder I was. Some things never change.

I guess these hikes deserve more than such a passing reference, so let me tell you a bit more about them. Having well worn my Czech hiking boots thumbing a thousand miles, when I "settled down" in Brno my feet were still itching. So, when I had a big block of time on my hands, I'd sometimes head off into the nearby hills and bang out another twenty sweaty miles.

These hilly forests were beautiful, and obviously well managed by a forester from the old school. Everything seemed healthy and in order. There was very little undergrowth, and even less fallen debris. Mature trees were spaced at respectable distances from each other — so it was easy to see for quite some distance through the woods. The herds of deer could run, but not really hide. The trails were wide and well-marked ... and yet abandoned. I never once met another two-footed soul on these hikes. Which was fine by me.

The trail system was so extensive and varied, that I rarely hiked exactly the same way twice. One chilly winter morning I was charging up an unfamiliar trail; breathing deeply and filling my lungs with oxygen fresh from the evergreens as I clipped along at a brisk pace. Suddenly, the air changed and I tasted something bitter and metallic as I exhaled; and my mind was somehow, here in the middle of a forest, brought back to the industrial darkness of Hodonín. I slowed a bit, but continued on toward the ridgetop ahead of me. As I reached the peak, I looked down at the valley and farmland before me. And at a little forgotten village of three hundred souls or so that looked (from a distance at least) exactly as it did when Napoleon's forces moved though these parts. The buildings were almost all painted a dull shade of yellow, with white and orange accents. These buildings all seemed about the same size, except for one near the center standing above the pack.

The village was compact, as they ought to be, and seemed to be ringed with a fence enclosure. Outside this enclosure, there was nothing but fields surrounded by high hills ... one of which concealed a silent witness from another world.

On any other day, it would have been an idyllic scene. But on that windless winter day a cloud of orange-gray smoke squatted over this little hamlet, and seemed to prevent it from communicating with the heavens above. The cloud was well-defined, and came nowhere near me on that far-away ridgetop. Nonetheless, its invisible residue was obviously all around me, since the familiar metallic taste on my tongue was from the sulphuric brown coal that these villagers all burned to stay warm.

Needless to say, childhood respiratory disease was endemic in Moravia. But at least frostbite was not.

Deerstand Dreams

How easy it is
to slip, to fall.
To Fall, and fear the land.

Land of earth which means no harm
Yet stands opposed, and will not yield.
I take small share of rushing wind
To fill small space and close to heart.

But hard hard earth compels a cough
To nourish thoughtless watching leaves.

Like many Czechs, Frank and I had only the tiniest of refrigerators in our apartment. So we were obliged to stop every other day or so at the small grocery store around the corner.

Grocery stores in Czechoslovakia were, according to the East Germans and Romanians I had met, unbelievable horns of plenty where one could find anything and everything: "Meat, coffee, vegetables, canned goods, you name it!" My American perspective was somewhat different. True, there *was* coffee — but only one brand and in one size: a package of whole beans that would last you less than a week. But, I must admit, you *could* find just about whatever you really needed, and usually less than 20% of the shelves were empty. I had spent enough time in East Germany — where I had seen entire walls of empty shelves guarded by empty clerks — to know why the rest of the East Bloc envied the wealthy Czechs.

As I carried a rusty mesh shopping basket around my local *potraviny* I picked up, along with my essentials, lessons in Comintern trade. Though 95% of the products came from Eastern Europe, my American eyes were especially drawn to the misfits from continents afar: Rum from Cuba, and rice from Vietnam.

Many brand names were simple derivatives of their country of origin, and most of the products were packaged very plainly with logos or artwork in the Spartan style of socialist realism. Some packages had nothing but three words and a solitary red star on them. One bag featured a colored pencil portrait of an androgynous farm laborer staring blankly toward the horizon, his/her arms full of grain. A golden hammer and sickle for a halo floating over that sexless head.

The industrial and industrious Czechs produced lots of high-quality products (troop transports, aircraft, machine guns, spy cameras, bugging devices, etc.) that all of the world's Communist governments lusted for. So naturally Czechoslovak grocery stores were relatively full of the simple foodstuffs those governments could offer in return.

I've just moved to Brno, a great old city right in the center of CSFR. There is a certain spot in Brno that some locals claim to be the center of the world. You see, Brno's in the center of CSFR, CSFR is in the center of Europe, and of course Europe is the center of the world. I call them "Brnocentrists."

Don gave me a sort of welcome tour of the English Department's real estate and, without realizing it, gave me some vague insights into the way things had worked there eight months prior when someone less Canadian ran the show.

Don was such an optimistic and happy sort that the evils of Communism were virtually invisible to him. And those he could not avoid seeing became, in his eyes, merely humorous foibles. Things one could laugh about if one had to notice them. *But really, it's better not to notice these things … life is short! Focus on more productive things and don't get sidetracked with silly negativity. Really now!*

He showed me the lockable glass bookcases where certain books were kept, and the request slips one needed to fill out to gain access to these. Perhaps this system was merely to prevent theft, but something seemed odd to me about these books behind glass. Not *all* of the faculty's books were locked away, but some were. Who decided what went where, and why? Was this merely a dry calculation of material value? I don't think so.

But Don chose not to ask these pointless questions, and just went on about his happy life … blessed to live in the heart of Europe with the woman he loved and surrounded by books. *Could I possibly have it any better?!*

He had a similarly beautiful blindness about the people he knew, including me. I don't think Don ever hated another human being, or saw the black spots on their souls. Dark blots which seemed painfully obvious to me. He sometimes laughed at human weakness, but not in an unkind way. It was all just part of the glorious *Comedia Divina*.

Isn't life grand?! Really, isn't it?! Oh, if only this joy could go on forever! Of course it cannot, but let's not talk about that, OK? Life is beautiful! Say that in any language you choose, it's still true.

Don showed me the well-lit faculty break-room on the top floor: a 20'x20' living room of sorts with armchairs and bookcases and lamps and coffee tables strewn neatly with scholarly journals from England. There he introduced me quickly to a few people who would later become my friends but who, in that moment, were still just nameless faces. Even though Don *had* of course just told me their names.

We left the break-room and took a left, heading down a poorly lit hallway toward its abrupt end. Then we looked left toward a heavy wooden door with a blue plastic nameplate affixed to it announcing that this room belonged to one *"Milada Franková."* Don apologized sincerely that my name was not yet on the door, but promised me he'd take steps to fix that shortcoming soon … as if I actually cared.

He swung open the door and showed me the spacious office I'd soon share with Milada and where, he told me, I'd need to plant myself during certain set hours so that students could come to see me if they needed to. I saw yet another glass bookcase, and a bright though dusty window overlooking the heart of Europe. I walked slowly over to "my" window, and looked out over the timeless God-fearing architecture of Czechoslovakia's infancy.

And thought to myself, "Could I *possibly* have it any better? Really, could I?! *Non sum dignum.*"

It wasn't until the next day that I was blessed to put a face to the blue name on my door.

Milada greeted me with a beautiful smile that filled her whole being. Or rather one that radiated from the core of that being and said clearer than words, *"I am so glad to meet you! And so glad we will soon become friends. Of course we really are friends already but still, it's going to be such fun sharing this office with you. I'm so glad you came!"*

Milada was, and is, a serious scholar. She has published dozens of lengthy articles in academic journals printed not only in her homeland, but in many other countries too. These articles are, of course, written in English. Absolutely perfect, beautiful English. The same English I heard her speak virtually every working day.

I found it almost impossible to recall that she had *not* spoken that language her entire life.

Milada was highly intelligent, well-read, and cultured. But those are not terribly rare qualities really. Neither are they terribly important in the grand scheme of things. What *was* more unique about Milada, *and* more important in that grand scheme, was that heart of hers. A heart so full of kindness, respect, and *joie de vivre* that I can never forget the hundreds of happy hours I spent within six feet of its radiating warmth. She really was, and is, a saint of sorts in my mind.

I can clearly picture her reading the words I just wrote and laughing kindly while thinking to herself, *"Oh Mark, you're such a silly young man. You really romanticize everything, don't you?!"* While instead of voicing those words which might be hurtful she simply says to me, "Oh Mark, you're much too kind. But thank you dear. That's very sweet of you." Smiling all the while and radiating her inherent holiness — completely unaware that she was doing so.

We never discussed her personal life really, but I believe that she had children just a little younger than I was at the time. Most of what I know about Milada I inferred, since she seemed to live by the wise old adage *me me me is dull dull dull.* We spoke a little bit about ideas and literature; quite a bit about language and culture; but mostly about harmless niceties like the weather and tram rides and tea.

It took a while before I inferred that Don had hired her just a few months before he hired me — I had at first assumed she'd been there for her entire career. I never asked, and so never learned, why she had first made it onto the faculty at the age of forty-something right after the Velvet Revolution. Coincidence? Or was she unwelcome before then? Was there some very un-red blot on her that made her *non grata* under the Reds? I honestly still have no idea.

I do know that at some point in the mid-60's, before the Russians fixed things in freewheeling Czechoslovakia, she had lived in England. And I also know that such "distinctions" were not particularly appreciated by the authorities.

My romantic nature — the one Milada would silently chide me for (while just as silently finding it endearing) — makes me prefer to imagine that there *was* something about Milada that the Reds found untrustworthy.

They would have been right, of that I am sure.

Milada liked to think of me, I think, as a son. It saddens me a little to realize that she is now old enough to have grandchildren as old as I was then, and that I am now almost as old as she was when I knew *her*. As the simple folk would ask, *where does the time go?* Really … where? I'd like to ask Aristotle that one someday.

Following this idea of Milada as my Czech mother, I'd like to explore the sterner side of this saint's character. It started off with subtle hints, but gradually worked its way up to ill-disguised consternation. "Mark, *WHEN* are you going to shave properly?!"

I couldn't even consider retorting to my beloved mother-in-stead, "When you Czechs, who somehow manage to manufacture jet aircraft and some of the most finely machined rifles in the world, finally figure out how to put a sharp edge on a friggin' razor blade!" Instead, I just shrugged and smiled guiltily as if to say *sorry Mom!*

This subject of my haggard appearance was the only subject that ever prompted Milada to address me with anything less than loving kindness, so it obviously was an important one to her. It was in fact her repeated questioning that finally prompted me, toward the end of that first semester, to throw in the steamy towel and grow a proper beard. Which perhaps, as an added bonus, went well with the professorial persona I was attempting to affect at that time.

The pretty girls that I kissed didn't seem to care either way. So what the hell, why not?

I quickly adapted well to my new environment, and quickly fell into a new daily routine. After morning classes I'd walk a block or two to a small soup bar — where I could order any one of a dozen different soups on the menu.

I still at that point spoke very little Czech beyond "hello" and "thank you" so I'd just look up at the handwritten menu on the chalkboard, pick any random selection there, and read it to the server as best I could manage. Sometimes I'd have to repeat myself, but for the most part I made myself understood. Of course *I* never understood what I was saying, but that didn't matter – lunch was about to be served.

My selection was served to me in a large bowl on a plastic tray that also had a long bread roll sliding around on it randomly. I had to grab a spoon myself, then place my tray on one of three chest-high stainless steel tables. Half the patrons ate standing, but I usually chose to grab one of the tall steel stools and plant myself atop it.

There definitely was a protocol there, and I'm pretty sure I followed it: Don't rush, but don't take up any more time than you need; don't take any more *room* than you need, don't bump anyone with your tray, don't get any soup on your tray. *Do* dump your breadcrumbs in the garbage, please, and always say thank you.

This routine worked pretty well for me and I slowly did learn a few new Czech words in the process: lentil, corn, potato, celery, tomato, and tripe. I actually learned to *like* tripe soup, and ordered that one on purpose several times.

One day, I noticed a new name on the menu and sounded it out confidently, *"Jedna krvavá polévka prosím."*

When I sat down on my stool I studied the dark greasy blobs floating atop and throughout my soup with apprehension. Something was not right in the state of Denmark, of that I was quite sure. Nonetheless, I took a large spoonful of the stuff and downed it. Then chased it quickly with a bite of bread. I was determined to get down the medicine I had so proudly ordered for myself, and to *keep* it down, but I just barely managed to do so.

Mission accomplished, I cleaned the crumbs off my tray, said thank you, and headed back to my office.

When I got there I asked Milada, "What exactly is *krvavá polévka?*"

"Oh, that's blood soup!" she replied with that kind smile of hers.

I just barely managed a half-smile back as I said, "Yeah, that's kinda what I thought."

Another routine that I fell into quickly upon settling in Brno was a weekly visit to my favorite early find there: the antiquarian bookshop near Freedom Square. The place was loaded with thousands of leather-bound and dusty treasures. Books that had been printed long before Robespierre had lopped a single Parisian head – i.e. back when hedonistic kings still ate cake with their mistresses while their wives made witty comments in a room just three hundred yards down the hall.

That bookstore was, for me, an oasis where I could imagine that modernity had never paved the world. And where I could steal priceless treasures at will.

Aromatic works of theology in German, history in Latin, and literature in French were there by the dozens. Along with ink-penned liturgical music with penciled-in notes, ancient Roman Missals stained with drops of sacramental wine, and Brevariae with pressed flowers from past centuries stuck between their pages. Any of the above and more could be yours for roughly four dollars each.

That was of course a full day's pay, and a lot of money, in the Czechoslovakia of 1990. So the shop's manager seemed completely indifferent each time I brought yet another dusty volume over to the register. It was just business, and what could be more harmless than business?

Still, I felt a pang of guilt each time; knowing that I was robbing this poor nation of national treasures, and that these treasures would ultimately end up half-read and resting on a dry bookshelf in the New World. I wondered what other national treasures, greater than these, were being stolen by my wealthier compatriots at the same time. I still don't know, and would rather not. Please, don't tell me.

Though there was certainly plenty of back-room intrigue at Versailles before that place was turned into a museum, nothing in history, that I know of, could compare to the intrigues that took place under Communism.

We may never know the exact extent of commonplace duplicity during the Communist era, but one of my students told me that one in ten Czech adults had been on the payroll of the secret police. Exaggerated? Probably. But total control requires total knowledge. An authoritarian regime simply needs to watch the troublemakers. A totalitarian regime is obsessed with watching everyone, all the time.

My anti-communist informant informed me that every single workplace had at least one imbedded spy. Should the English Department of a university be any different? Hardly! It took me all of forty-eight hours in my new position to sniff her out.

The faculty of the Department was a very aristocratic yet

democratic bunch. Most of these Czechs spoke British English much better than an average Londoner. They could have blended into a conversation at Oxford unnoticed. And they could have spoken about the same things people talked about at Oxford in the 1960's: like, maybe, the odd occasional echo of Nietzche's philosophy in the Beatles' lyrics.

Though exceptionally cultured, they were not stuffy in the least. They had a great deal of genuine affection for each other, and you could picture almost any one of them hugging any other – except for our one wrinkled toad.

She smiled all the time, stretching her creased skin tight around her round face. She laughed at her own jokes, which were never funny. She hugged a two-foot stack of paperwork as she marched down the hallway on her way to class; whereas everyone else carried one small folder under the arm. She seemed to avoid the faculty break room, where everyone else sat telling jokes that *were* funny.

Everyone on the faculty tolerated her, except for my friend and distinguished colleague, Mirek Pospíšil.[*] You could tell, he hated her. Mirek had been part of the underground intelligentsia, and used to meet secretly with philosophers from England when they came to town.

Mirek was Czech of course, but I often forgot that – mistaking him for upper-crust British. His command of the English language was, I'm quite sure, better than mine. He was tall and handsome, about forty years old, and had slightly long brown hair. He usually dressed in a turtleneck and sport coat, and pretty much looked like what he was: a pre-Deconstructionist intellectual of the highest caliber; a throwback to happier days in the Western intellectual tradition.

---

[*] Mirek might be the one exception to my "not stuffy in the least" comment. But I did not, and do not, hold that against him in the slightest. He had an awful lot of crap to rise above in his day, and adopting a British air of confident superiority was probably a pretty good way to do that.

One day, about four of us were in the hallway having a conversation about the Gulf War (the first one — kicking Hussein out of Kuwait). Mirek was drawing parallels to 1938, when most of the world felt that the sovereignty of itty-bitty Czechoslovakia was not worth fighting for. And as soon as he had made that connection, our toad-in-residence suddenly hopped into our midst, from out of nowhere, and interjected with wide eyes and a tight half-smile, "I hope this war will be over *soon!*"

My normally reserved friend blasted back at her with hellfire in his eyes, "It'll be *over* when it's <u>*over!!*</u>"

Our scolded informant pulled her lips in tight toward her stained teeth, lifted her eyebrows even higher than usual, and hopped away clutching her all-important stack of papers tight to her broad bosom. Surely depressed to realize that she had nothing to gain by reporting this outburst, since her StB connections didn't matter anymore. Nor, for that matter, did she.

Another friend I made on the faculty was another Pospíšil … Tomaš. (I suppose "Pospíšil" is something like the Czech equivalent of "Smith." But I assure you, it's much harder to write on an American keyboard.)

Tomaš was only a few years older than me, and a very junior member of the faculty on the long road toward professorship. He was often unshaven — obviously sharing my disdain for brutally dull Czech razor blades.

Tomaš had a pleasant smile, an easy demeanor, and a very curious mind with a slightly muted aspect of intensity. That intensity would spark just enough to be intelligible when the conversation turned toward particularly esoteric subjects: like Shopenhauer's views on marriage; or Hawthorne's early life.

You could tell that he was particularly interested in what you had to say when his eyes opened wider and he dropped his head down and forward slightly. He gave me the benefit of that expression often — I think especially because his chosen field of expertise was Americana, and I represented to him an opportunity of study.

I suspect it distressed Tomaš that I cared more about Shakespeare and Schubert than Kerouac and kitsch. But nonetheless, he always gave me the impression that he liked me. I doubt he particularly did, but kind-hearted interest and genuine humanistic concern were things that came naturally to him – much more than they did to me.

Sometimes I'd make some random comment or other, and Tomaš would do that head and eye thing of his while asking, in sort of an American hippy slur, *"Really?!"*

"Yes, Tomaš, really … I guess. What did I say?"

I'm sure Tomaš has forgotten me, but as you can see I have not forgotten him. I hope to meet him again someday, and to give him a friendly dopeslap:

"Really, Tomaš, *Kerouac?* Dude, you can do better than that. I know you can. You're like, Czech – can't you dig that?

Journal Entry from September 13, 1990

"Man trying to be just a good animal always turns out to be so much worse than any other animal."

Cleanth Brooks

I felt like I had already comfortably fallen in place as the faculty's only American when I was suddenly joined by another. One who had all the qualifications I lacked: an honest-to-goodness PhD from an American university. So obviously a man oozing knowledge and wisdom from every pore.

Greg scared me the first time I met him. He looked a bit sweaty and nervous, and when he spoke he gritted his teeth and seemed to shake. I'm not sure if he actually *did* shake, but the faulty noises coming haltingly out of him betrayed the fact that his diaphragm was fighting against him. It protested pushing air outward to permit those words to spill from his mouth.

Every breath seemed laborious for Greg. Not at all on the intake, but very much so as it left him. It was as though the life-giving blessings of air were reluctant to leave him once they'd got inside. But he made them leave nonetheless, through a supreme effort of The Will; and he was clearly determined to keep up this painful process until that oxygen-laden air refused to enter him at all. Until the assembled molecules called *Greg* finally disintegrated into nothingness.

All of this I gleaned within five seconds. I never learned anything more significant about him, even though I saw him nearly every day for three semesters.

He always dressed head-to-toe in black, as if he were dressed for his own funeral. Or perhaps he was boasting that he was already dead, and that he himself had been the executioner. He had sacrificed his own soul at the unholy temple of learning, and was proud to show the world what a noble, selfless thing he had done for our sakes.

I think most of the students found Greg much more interesting than they did me, and they flocked to special lectures he gave in unlit rooms. In part because there they would get to watch clips from American movies, and hear inner-city rap music pounding from a big boom box. This beat the pants off of Shakespeare, no doubt.

I never went to one of his lectures, though I attended many others given by visiting scholars from England. In fact, this probably does not surprise you, I made an effort to avoid them entirely.

The closest brush I had with one of Greg's lectures was the day I happened to be walking past one and heard the words *"I GOT THE POWER!!"* blasting over and over again from Greg's portable sound system.

I slowed my pace just a bit to figure out what was going on, and saw nearly every one of my students spread out all over the floor in there. The lights were off for some reason or other, and I could just barely hear Greg's shaky voice over the thumping beat. I could not make out what he was saying, but I'll bet I could have written that lecture myself if I had chosen to. It would have been full of the words, *phallocentric, power-structure, hegemony, disempowerment, disenfranchisement, disthisanddisthat.*

Lectures like that are really much easier to write than they seem. They are just hard to deliver when your diaphragm refuses to cooperate and to follow your brain's orders.

Greg ended up within two months of his arrival hooking up with a very attractive blonde I'd never seen before. She was not one of our students, so I don't know where he picked her up. He told me very proudly right after I first laid eyes on her that her parents had been Communist big-wigs before the revolution, as if that fact would make me even more envious. It did not.

Truly, I felt sorry for Greg even then; though I knew I could never express that sentiment to him. Neither could I do what I think he expected me to do: thank him. For abandoning any selfish hope for immortality, any happiness, any inner peace, and, any appreciation for anything at all. For eternally forswearing thoughtless and painless respiration. For selflessly sacrificing his so-called soul on the altar of modernity.

The least I could do, thought Greg, is say *thanks.* But no, Greg, no thanks. None still.

Journal Entry from September 27, 1990

Greg told me that he likes modern writing because it's "concrete." This is true, but I don't *like* concrete. I never considered the Berlin Wall a work of art.

I spent an awful lot of time in those days riding around on Brno's antique red trams. Not only because I needed to, but also because I liked to. One day, as I sat on a tram near my new home, I saw a uniformed soldier waiting for a bus.

Here he was, in the middle of a huge residential neighborhood and far from any military base, all by himself. And looking painfully sad and lonely. It took me several seconds to notice his emotional state and realize that this was in fact another human being, since I was at first distracted by his dark uniform and even more by his shiny boots: tall black "jack boots" of the sort I had only seen in Third Reich newsreels.

"Wow, a real-life *Wehrmachtsoldaten* risen from the dead!" Really, that *was* my first thought … *"Huh, a Nazi? Here? Now?"*

But then I studied his face and saw that he was little more than a boy. My age, at best. And I saw that he was in pain.

It took me just another two seconds to notice the red star on his hat. And I then realized where this love-sick kid was *really* from; and what he was really all about. He was the last gasp of *The Evil Empire*: A soldier from the Soviet Union coming to Russian Street, for the last time, to say goodbye to his Czech lover. Since the curtain had just been pushed several hundred kilometers eastward, and his commanding officers had ordered a retreat back to the Motherland.

That kid really was, all by himself, a poem without words.

In that first year after the Velvet Revolution, I was almost always the first American anyone had met. As such, I was something of a celebrity and in great demand. I was often invited out for drinks by an acquaintance, and when I got there would find another half-dozen strangers waiting for me, eager to speak with me and proud to practice their English.

On one of these evenings in September of 1990 I found myself in a very mixed group of six. Two of them I had already met: Daša (a young university student), and Miloš, a white-haired and bearded factory worker of about sixty-five. The other three were strangers to me, and somewhere between these two in ages.

We were at a dingy beer hall with dingy patrons and green fluorescent lighting. They served both *Plzeňský Prazdroj* and *Budvar* on tap — two of the oldest and best Czech beers. The six of us sat at a large booth, and everyone spoke only English, even though one guy had a very hard time of it.

It was a fun night, more or less. It *was* a little disconcerting to me to see that we were really bothering the regulars, who kept glancing at us with suspicious glinty eyes. I guess they didn't appreciate hearing laughter in juxtaposition with a language they could not comprehend. But who does?*

As we left that dark place, Miloš put his heavy hand on my shoulder, gave me a sly smile, and said, "My friend, it looks like *you* are in trouble!" I'm sure I looked just as confused as I felt even before he followed up with, "She's a *very* beautiful girl." Daša? I had never

---

* It's also worth mentioning that the presence of a "Westerner" often invoked dirty glances in those days – usually from pudgy individuals with gray wrinkled skin. I was used to those glances, and got them frequently on buses and trams. I should note further that they were only "glances" when the xenophobe was male. Women would glare and stare and try to burn a hole of hatred right through you. I remember staring back at one such woman once while I was seated on a tram in Brno with a French copy of Pascal's Pensées in my hand. She glared, and I stared; showing her that I saw right into her soul and that it wasn't a nice thing to see. This is one of few such anecdotes that I can put an exact date on, because that night (September 11, 1990) I wrote in my journal, "Look the Devil straight in the face – he hates when you do that."

noticed. And what … was she flirting with me? I hadn't noticed that either.

I have often experienced this in my life, especially in my interactions with women: a sudden shocking revelation that I am completely clueless.

The next time I saw Daša, I carefully studied her features and really saw her for the first time. "My God, she *is* beautiful!" I noticed for the first time that she had the type of face and figure favored on the runways of Paris and Milan — only slightly flawed and more human. And thus more beautiful.

She had jet-black hair and pale delicate skin. Her torso was very slim, with virtually no breasts to speak of. Her graceful legs and arms moved in subtle undulations, as if she gently floated through life on one of Chagall's canvases. She was one of God's rare masterpieces. Or the Devil's, depending on your perspective.

I saw Daša fairly often after that night, but still always in the company of others. Now that I was paying attention, I could see that she certainly *was* flirting with me — in the most subtle and innocent ways. I now made sure she received the same attention she'd been giving me all this time, and our eyes often connected a little longer than would be considered prudent in mixed company. Our eyes touched often, though our bodies never did. I do not believe we so much as shook hands.

When I first looked deep into her brown eyes with mine wide open, I saw something else I hadn't noticed before: A maturing soul in flux; with dreams, fears, and secret longings. Her soul's nascent and uncertain convictions searched mine for guidance — even in the distracting company of strangers.

A seemingly eternal fortnight of this deep communication passed before that night when I found myself alone with her in a room as if it were ordained. I had gone to a small party on the outskirts of the city, and there she was.

At one point, late in the evening, the last stranger finally left the room we were in. Daša was seated in front of me, slightly below me, and quartering away. The electricity of this momentous occasion ran through the two of us as we sat a foot apart in silence. We sat for a long while just relishing life; not looking at each other, not speaking, not doing *anything* but drink in this fresh new air like a sacred communion prepared just for us.

Then, without a word, I reached down, touched the back of her head, and massaged the skin behind her ears with my fingertips. As I did so, her shoulders dropped, and she took in a deep breath through her nose.

Since she was more or less facing away from me, I could just barely see her eyes close as her expression became blissful and relaxed. It gave me joy to see that I had brought her peace. I leaned down, put my lips beside her little ear, and breathed in the fine scent of my love.

After several seconds, she turned toward me and lifted her eyes to look up toward mine. Her face now bore a new expression: One that spoke of hope, desperation, joy, and sorrow all mixed into one.

She broke the divine silence we'd been drinking for so long with precisely two dozen words: "Mark, there's something I need to tell you. I don't know if you knew this, but I have a husband back in my hometown."

I felt a hammer flatten my heart with one well-placed blow.

I quickly processed Daša's shocking news as best I could with the distraction of her vulnerable face within inches of mine, and her delicate hand pressing gently on my upper chest. The sweet memories of our seemingly eternal courtship swam desperately in a salty new ocean of waves and tidal currents.

My mind spun in a whirlwind of unspoken questions. *"How is that possible, you're so young?* When do you even see him, you're always*

---

* I later began to understand that marrying at eighteen was the norm in Czechoslovakia. Since housing was hard to come by, and rationed by the State, the only way to be put on a ten-year waiting list for a place away from Mom & Dad was to get married. Most eighteen-year-olds simply married the person they happened to be dating in their senior year of high school. It wasn't about love,

here at school?! How could *I have known?! Was I supposed to have done more homework before letting myself fall in love with you?!"*

After five eternal seconds my heart, though still wounded, started to beat again and encouraged my brain to step aside. So I told Daša simply, in the kindest whisper I could muster, "No, I did not know that."

I removed my hand from the back of her head. And brought it up to the front. And then brought up my other hand too. I rubbed her smooth pale cheeks with my two thumbs, and gently pushed my fingertips back through her hair. Then approached her waiting lips, slowly, with mine.

---

romance, commitment, or even sex. It was just about hoping to get out of Mom & Dad's impossibly cramped apartment before turning thirty. I'm sure very often it was Mom who had first suggested, "You know, I think this would be a good year for you to get married and try to get a place of your own."

Again the sound of
ever ever evermore
stirs a feeling
felt before.

Two days later I walked into my office and Milada said, "Oh Mark, you just missed her. A *very* pretty girl was just here looking for you!" I had a good idea who she might be talking about, but I played dumb and asked casually, "Oh, really? One of my students?" She said, "I don't think so. I'm pretty sure she's not an English major … I've never seen her before." That nailed it … Daša … *my love.* My heart took an irregular beat, filled with guilty pleasure.

I had just finished my last class of the day, so I packed up and headed home. When I got there, I was surprised to notice Daša's stunning essence seated near my apartment building. She smiled, got up, and came over to me. I was so happy to see her, and to see her there. She had never been to my place but I *had* told her my address. She obviously remembered!

We went inside the building and as we climbed the stairs toward the door to my third floor apartment, she rubbed my lower back. She smiled so sweetly, and so completely, that I wanted to kiss her right there. But I decided to wait until we got inside the apartment. Once we were in, I grabbed her in my arms and kissed her wildly all over her face and neck. She reciprocated in a frenzy of kissing for a short while, then pushed me gently away with a smile. She took my hand in hers and led me around the place as if she knew where she was going. She brought me beside my bed, and without a word motioned for me to sit. She then backed up from me about two paces and, without taking her eyes off mine, started slowly unbuttoning her blouse.

I felt an intense rush of excitement. And then the fear of mortal danger. The phrase *"Thou Shall Not Commit Adultery"* rang with quaint power in my ears. I had to act and act quickly: I had to stop a supermodel from undressing herself in my bedroom … now!

I jumped up from the bed, pulled her hands off her shirt, and started slowly re-buttoning it with my clumsy fingers and thumbs. Her jaw dropped a little and she looked at my awkward hands with a confused stare as this odd New Englander went slowly about his puritanical business.

I then picked her up, and carried her to my bed. I laid her down on her back, and lay down beside her. I touched her face tenderly, and kissed her some more. (You see, I was perfectly content to *kiss* another man's wife. But "the forfended place" was just that. "No way, not gonna go there!")

As I kissed her she did not close her eyes all the way: she was watching me. She did allow me to kiss her for a long time, and even kissed me back … but it was different now.

The next afternoon I was alone with Daša again, and we walked down *Vodova ulice* holding hands. This is an old residential neighborhood, and at that time of day the street was virtually abandoned. But still, I wondered: wasn't she worried someone would see us? Couldn't word get back home? She seemed so nonchalant … and maybe a little distant. As we walked together I relished that beautiful, forbidden hand in mine and I studied the equally beautiful and even more forbidden body attached to it. Overcome with desire, I yanked her into a random covered doorway and kissed her hard, squeezing her slender body so tight I'm sure it hurt a little.

I brought her back to my apartment, led her to my bed, and pushed her down onto it with firm gentleness. I kissed her all over her face and neck, and studied her remarkable beauty from up close. Then, the stone tablets from on high — which had motivated me so powerfully just 24 hours prior – suddenly dissolved: I decided I'd have her then and there.

I reached down to touch her breast. But she grabbed my hand and pushed it away. I made another move for her nether regions, but she intercepted me again.

I wondered bitterly, "Is this the same girl who was so anxious to give herself to me yesterday?" No, it was not. This new girl was perfectly content to *kiss* a man not her husband but …

Our next date went pretty much the same way and then it was over. Our relationship was leading neither to marriage nor illicit sex … so what was the point?

Our souls, which had communicated so eloquently before we had ever touched, had nothing more to say.

Can a woman ever really understand a man? Men can't understand women and they're proud to say so. A woman often thinks she's got us all figured out … but does she? I don't think so. If she really knew us to our cores she wouldn't want us … and vice versa.

ELEISON

Mercy, Mercy, Mercy
Thrice begged in rolling r's.
Undeserved but all the same
asked, asked, asked.

Passing a large stone church with clean exterior lines, a colorful note pinned to its front door caught my eye. I approached and saw three hand-drawn flags in primitive magic marker: German, French, and British. Beside the Union Jack four words were spelled out carefully in blocky letters: "ENGLISH SPOKEN HERE. WELCOME!"

I felt my fate cry out so I pressed, then pulled, on the heavy wooden door. It would not budge. I tried the door on the other side but it was locked as well. Undeterred, I sat down on stones worn smooth by twenty generations of faithful feet and wrote a simple note:

Dear Father,
I am an American living here in Brno, and I would like to join the Holy Mother Church. Please write to me at 10 Ruská, Královo Pole. Thank you —

Mark A. Brallier

I slipped the paper into an iron box and continued on my way, feeling lighter of heart than I had in a long while.

I watched my mail with greater-than-usual expectation for a week, having no doubt whatsoever that one day soon my prayers would be answered. On the seventh day, a postcard arrived. It bore a simple photograph of a landscape near Pardubice, but it looked to me like the familiar Berkshire Hills of Massachusetts: A rolling hayfield with a solitary oak tree in the middle, and a mixed forest of birch, beech, and cedar around its distant periphery. The postcard's colors were faded and slightly untrue — just like the ancient colors of my Kodachrome youth.

I flipped the card over and saw crooked off-center typewriter print like my grandfather used to bang out in his study while I played in the hayfields:

Brno, Octber 25th90

Hallo. dear Mark!
Than'k you very much for your paper in our
Jesuit church.We'd love to meet you and
to speak to you - please. visit us in our
Church after the Eucharist
/Daily at 12.15 and 18.00 -
Sunday 7.30 9.30 and 21.00

*this week there is no evening Mass
at Wedn and Friday.*

Fr Joseph Blaha SJ

I attended lunchtime Mass on a random weekday, and then after most everyone else had left I confidently approached the man who had just broken bread for the three dozen elderly ladies there with me.

Father Josef greeted me with a powerful two-handed handshake and a big smile. He spoke quickly in an English unlike any I had ever heard. Perfectly comprehensible, but with an accent, timbre, and rhythm all its own. His taste in music and his singing voice would later lead me to believe he had been born completely tone deaf, and I suspect this aural handicap affected his speech in all five of his other languages as well — but I never had the ability to test that theory.

We spoke for thirty minutes or so about just about everything imaginable: history, politics, academics, languages, etc. Perhaps the only subject we did not cover was the details of Catholic conversion, and we became great friends.

The following Sunday after Mass my new friend approached me quickly. (He did everything quickly, as if the deadline of mortality was never far from his busy thoughts.) "Are you free now?" he asked as he grasped my right hand. "Great, let's go have lunch!"

We left the cool dimness of his church and rushed into the bright light outdoors without even a moment to allow our eyes to adjust. I then learned that Father Josef walked even faster than he spoke. I squinted and kept up with him without difficulty, realizing that I was in the company of a man with intense purpose and realizing that, should I find such purpose too, I was more than capable of moving through life at Josef's speed.

Now in street clothes and without the collar I had grown to expect, there was nothing to tell the outside world that Josef was a priest. And I think that's the last thing anyone would have taken him for. An athletic, masculine, and confident man of about thirty, he didn't fit the stereotype at first glance – and even less so when he spoke. He was essentially a perfectly normal man with a mischievous sense of humor and wide-ranging, diverse passions. I imagine priests like him were common in centuries past, but I personally haven't met another since I said goodbye to him sixteen years ago.

My new friend and I hustled through *Naměsti Svobody* and wound our way uphill toward Peter and Paul cathedral, one of two dominating features in Brno's skyline (the other being *Špilberk*, the yellow-walled fortress that overlooks Brno and its surroundings).

As we finished our quick ascent, Josef lead me through a narrow passageway, and then through a small secret door which took us into the bishop's grand residence. This centuries-old palace was deserted and completely silent. We finally slowed our pace, since every footstep interrupted the sublime peace of the place. I think even Josef's handicapped ears could appreciate that.

As we walked down a hallway running along an exterior wall, I glanced out of the windows at the glorious views, including a close-up of the *dom* on Petrov hill from an angle I'd never seen before. This neo-Gothic cathedral in dark brown stone sits proudly atop the city; and one is always, even after climbing the hill it rests on, looking up at it uncomfortably. But from this unusual vantage point the church and I seemed to see eye-to-eye.

Josef and I turned a corner and entered a very large room with tapestries on the walls and dinner seating for seventy-five souls or so. Narrow dining tables were arranged neatly in a large rectangle mirroring the perimeter of the room. Huge floor-to-ceiling windows spaced along the long wall opposite us shed brilliant defused light throughout the room, and would have enlivened whatever large gathering should have been there. We were the only ones present.

Josef motioned for me to sit, and then left me alone briefly to observe my surroundings. He returned quickly, somehow, with two steaming bowls of soup, two elongated rolls, and two oversized spoons. He placed all of this in front of us, said a quick prayer, and then we started to eat our first meal together.

This simple meal, in this uncommon location and in this uncommon company, would soon become my Sunday routine.

I was, as I indicated, wholly unqualified to be teaching English in a university. True of course from a technical perspective, since I did not have a PhD … nor even a Master's for that matter. But I was in over my head from a purely practical perspective as well, since my knowledge of English grammar was (and still is) purely intuitive. Somehow the people charged with educating me did not feel that old-fashioned grammar lessons meant anything anymore. Likewise consigned to the dustbins of history: Latin, Greek, and Christ.

I made the best of a bad situation by following textbooks designed for dummies like me: teachers whose sole qualification was having heard English coming at them through the bars of their crib. In truth, my students already knew much more about the structure of my language than I ever will, and would sometimes ask me questions about the "dative case" or some similar mystery. "'*Dative?*' That's a bit personal, isn't it?"

They of course pretty quickly figured out that I had no idea what I was doing — so decided to use their time with me exploring differences between American and British vernacular, and learning what they could about the so-called culture of my homeland.

I know that the lessons they had for me were far more valuable than the ones I had for them; and I'm pretty sure they knew it too.

Soon after I started my new job, Don handed me a document that the university bureaucrats had prepared for me. It was printed on thin translucent paper and bore a stamp in blue ink, and another one in red ink.

Czechoslovakia was the land of rubber stamps. There were stamps for everything … old-fashioned wooden ones of the sort you can still see occasionally in rural American post offices. Certain paper pushers loved their stamp collections with a passion, and enjoyed nothing more than the exquisitely sexual process of getting that thing good and wet on a slippery ink pad before lifting it like a scepter and bringing it down cleanly and firmly on a piece of virgin paper, blotting it with their mark for all time and for all to see. Letting the power of the almighty State flow through their unworthy yet somehow sanctified hands.

This particular piece of paper proved that I was an employee of that State in good standing, and I was supposed to bring this document down to the regional police headquarters to be registered as such.

I'm sure you know enough about me by now to know that I did no such thing. I thanked Don, stuck this ticket to legitimacy into one of my books of English literature, and went on about my life.

About a month later I did find myself walking by Brno's huge "VB" headquarters (which sits, strangely, near the prestigious Janáček Organ School). And I did pause for just a moment to wonder if maybe I should pop in there some day to say hello to the local cops. *Nah.*

Those were blessed days of peaceful anarchy in Czechoslovakia. Every day laws were being changed in Prague, and the rest of the country just quietly sat on the sidelines waiting for things to settle down before figuring out which laws were supposed to be enforced and which were not. To see which of the old ones would stick around and which would go away. In the meantime, don't take anything too seriously and just don't worry about things too much … it'll all work out.

I went with that free flow with all my heart and kept right on walking past that former house of ill repute and allowed its gray and green inhabitants to sulk inside without worrying about what sort of files, if any, they were now supposed to maintain on American citizens.

This passing spirit of anarchy was another reason that I didn't sweat the details when Frank told me that it was illegal to possess a firearm in Czechoslovakia unless you had special "papers" for it. Papers which were very hard to obtain if you had not *already* obtained papers proclaiming you a consecrated member of the Communist Party.

Yeah, sure, like they are really going to arrest me now? I don't think so.

When Frank and I left Brno to spend a weekend at his parents' little wooden dacha in the Moravian hills, I fearlessly stuffed the *St. Etienne* into my backpack, brought it with me on the bus, and practiced with it in the dacha's backyard. I quickly got so good with it that I could hit a five-crown coin from a distance of fifty feet, and put a clean hole right through the Communist star on its tail side.

I could see distress stamped on Frank's face when I showed him my accomplishment. *That's real money, Mark. My country's money.*

Sorry about that Frank, I just had to do it. I'd been waiting my whole life to do that.

After a full weekend of paying Rambo in the hills, I returned to the city the play professor.

As for this faux-professor thing I'd like to mention that, although I was neither as smart nor as well-educated as my students, they treated me very kindly. That's to say, as an equal.

There were no faculty rules against fraternization, and more than a few times I found myself enjoying the glories of Czech beer with my students. Even Don, the fifty-year-old head of our department, seemed very much at ease sharing a drink with these articulate and cultured kids.

One night, we did just that. Don and I were the only faculty members amongst a dozen or so students stumbling around Freedom Square shortly before midnight, and there seemed no imperative to maintain any distance between us. We were just a group of friends out having a good time. One of us happened to be a white-haired Canadian who had studied at Oxford, and another a twenty-something American who had been half-educated at a mid-rate State school. The rest, a bunch of Czech kids who had recently done well for themselves in high school, and happened to have a knack for languages. A few of these kids came from privileged Communist families, but most had much humbler backgrounds ... having grown up in concrete cells just like the one I used to pray in when I lived down in Hodonín. I think one of them actually was *from* Hodonín.

I don't know who started it, or why, but suddenly I found myself singing lustily in Latin with two of these kids.

"Confutatis! Maladictis! Flammis acribus addictis. Confutatis! Flammis acribus addictis!"

I sang the bass line, while one of my friends took the baritone and yet another the tenor.

I doubt this sort of thing happens spontaneously even at Harvard, where beer-buzzed undergraduates really *should* spout such rich esoterica. Maybe it does happen at Yale, but of course I wouldn't know — the bastards wouldn't let me in.

After my young friends and I were done with our bizarre revelry, Don approached me and asked, "What was that?" It was clear that he recognized the tune but couldn't quite place it.

"Mozart's Requiem."

"Oh, nice."

It just so happened we were walking past a building that Wolfgang once slept in, but I'm sure that was just a coincidence. Or was it?

November 1990 was a magical month. Around the first of the month, when Czechs I knew started talking about their first anniversary of freedom, that talk of time seemed surreal to me: I felt like I'd been living in Czechoslovakia forever, and it was hard to grasp that the Velvet Revolution had begun less than one year earlier. Even harder to grasp that I hadn't been there that entire year – not even close! I guess it's similar to the phenomenon athletes experience when a pivotal moment in a critical game arrives … it happens in slow motion and every detail burns itself indelibly in the memory. 1990, for me, seemed to span a decade.

If that year seemed to last so long for me, how much longer for the Czechs and Slovaks? The key events of the Velvet Revolution spanned only *ten days*, though I imagine those ten days must have seemed like forty years.

It all began on November 17, 1989 when a group of students organized under the aegis of "The Socialist Union of Youth" gathered in the streets of Prague to commemorate the death of a fellow college student who had been killed by the Nazis way back when.

No non-Socialist groups were *permitted* to gather in the streets of course, and, though this gathering had official sanction, it seems the authorities were somewhat suspect from the start. With good reason.

Because that small gathering of "Socialists" soon grew to be 15,000 strong and evolved into an overtly anti-Communist protest. Most of this "socialist" group's members announced proudly and publicly on that day that they were, in fact, freedom-lovers buoyed by the news that the Berlin Wall had just fallen.

The emboldened students were then corralled by riot police who blocked all escape routes. With the trap set, the well-paid enforcers moved in, with their hard batons, to teach these uppity punks a lesson in civics. When the exits were finally opened, hundreds of bleeding students scrambled away.

All except for one, who lay dead on the street for everyone to see … until three men finally dragged his limp corpse to shelter. News of the dead student spread like wildfire throughout the country, and ignited the fearless passion that soon undid the Communist regime.

This last part of the story, the dead student, remains one of the many mysteries of modern Czech history. We now know that his name was … I should say "is" … Ludvík Zifčák. We now know that he was only *playing* dead, and that he was a member of the secret police. And that the guys who dragged him away were *also* secret policemen.

Why did he do this? Was he put up to it? Or was he just scared and unable to tell the adrenaline-fueled riot police that he was one of them? Did he play dead just to save himself a few undeserved blows and thus, accidentally, did he help his country out of chains — and himself out of a job? We may never know.

All we do know is that in the popular mind Zifčák became a martyr with a new, fictional name. The demonstrations kept happening every day, and the 15,000 soon grew to 500,000. Huge peaceful gatherings happened not only in Prague, but in Brno, Bratislava, and several other cities as well. It soon became clear to Prague's Communist rulers that they had lost their ability to intimidate, and thus were no longer in control. And so, since their Russian puppeteers had made it clear that there would be no tanks propping them up *this* time round, they simply gave up.

Six weeks after Ludvík Zifčák played dead on a Prague street, Václav Havel delivered this "New Year's Address to the Nation" as its new president:

> *For forty years on this day you heard, from my predecessors, variations on the same theme: how our country flourished, how many million tons of steel we produced, how happy we all were, how we trusted our government, and what bright perspectives were unfolding before us.*
> *I assume you did not propose me for this office so that I, too, would lie to you.*

He went on from there to paint a depressing picture of a ravaged national landscape of injustice, ugliness, illness, and pollution.

> *But all this is still not the main problem. The worst thing is that we live in a contaminated moral environment. We fell morally ill because we got used to saying something different from what we thought. We learned not to believe in anything, to ignore each other, to care only for ourselves. Concepts such as love, friendship, compassion, humility, and forgiveness lost their depth and dimensions, and for many of us they came to represent only psychological peculiarities, or to resemble long-lost greetings from ancient times, a little ridiculous in the era of computers and spaceships ...*
> *I am talking about all of us. We had become used to the totalitarian system and accepted it as an unalterable fact of life, and thus we helped to perpetuate it. In other words we were all – though naturally to differing extents – responsible for the operation of totalitarian machinery. None of us is just its victim: we are also its co-creators ... we must accept this legacy as a sin we committed against ourselves.*

Can you imagine what was going through Ludvík Zifčák's mind when he heard these words?! He had unwittingly helped to unleash a man from outer space on his own country!

The next month, in February of 1990, this same alien landed in Washington D.C. At the time, I was still living in D.C. and hardly knew who Havel was. He addressed a joint session of the U.S. Congress and had a similar effect on that gathering of vainglorious hired guns as he did on Zifčák and his ilk: it was as if a Martian had dropped into their midst. Or perhaps more like Jefferson had risen from the dead to shame them by his example:

Consciousness precedes Being, and not the other way around, as Marxists claim. For this reason, the salvation of the human world lies nowhere else than in the human heart, in the human power to reflect, in human modesty, in human responsibility … responsibility to the order of Being, where all our actions are indelibly recorded and where, and only where, they will be properly judged.
The interpreter or mediator between us and this higher authority is what is traditionally referred to as human conscience.
If I subordinate my political behavior to this imperative, I can't go far wrong. If, on the contrary, I am not guided by this voice, not even ten presidential schools with two thousand of the best political scientists in the world could help me.

Knowing that they were on camera, the bewildered politicians tried not to look puzzled as they listened to this odd fellow spouting ideas that were either from outer space or perhaps just an ancient irrelevant era — they couldn't quite figure out which.

When he finished, they could do nothing but stand and clap, furiously, pretending they had actually understood what Havel had just said. And the few who really *did* understand his message accomplished an even greater stretch: pretending they had agreed with him. Havel has a gift for bringing out the best in everybody.

Around sunrise on the morning of November 17, 1990, I boarded a bus for Prague with a Slovak girl I hardly knew. Her name was Pavla, and she was one of my many students in the private language school where I moonlighted for extra unneeded crowns. Though she was quite attractive, I had no romantic interest in her. Nor she in me: we had just somehow started to spend a little time together outside the classroom, and somehow decided we'd celebrate the first anniversary of the Velvet Revolution together with two million friends in Prague.

My two-week-old relationship with her was still strangely platonic and tensionless; completely free of any expectations or even questions. You might say it was completely free of thought.

The bus was crammed full, and the passengers and driver chatted excitedly. Everyone knew that this was no ordinary day, and no ordinary bus ride. In a short two hours, Prague Castle showed itself through the windscreen, shining in the morning sun and towering over the city. Everyone fell speechless for a moment, as if our arrival signified something historic. Perhaps it did for me.

Pavla and I spent the whole morning wandering around a superlatively beautiful city that we both knew reasonably well already. The streets were much busier than I had ever seen them, packed as they were with other wanderers. Makeshift carnival-like displays and banners were everywhere. Some of these made fun of former Communist leaders — like the one showing Husák, the Czech president and Russian puppet, giving Comrade Brezhnev a passionate kiss on the lips. Another huge placard seemed to deify John Lennon with completely innocent sincerity.

Which brings me to an odd subject I have to address somewhere, so might as well get it over with now: Beatles songs in Czechoslovakia, in 1990, seemed perfectly in tune with the times. Everyone loved them without a hint of nostalgia — nobody thought of them as "oldies." It was as if popular culture had gone into hibernation when the tanks rolled in '68 and had awakened twenty-two years later with no sense of time lost. There was a naïve innocence about it too: like nobody knew that LSD even existed, or that disco had ever happened. It was surreal … and lovely.

The jammed streets buzzed with conversation – much less than 1% of which was conducted in English. I could pick out American voices only very occasionally, so this was nothing like Paris, where Americans shout at each other from opposite sides of every street.

So yes, there were *some* Americans besides me in Prague that day, but not enough to notice unless (like me) you were really paying attention. But nobody could have missed the American flags — they were everywhere. A few large ones flapped from poles or draped from windows, but tens of thousands of smaller ones bobbed down the street in Czech and Slovak hands. It made me feel uncomfortable, as if I suddenly had something much bigger to live up to than I'd really like to. I wanted to enjoy myself anonymously that day, but seeing all those flags made me feel like this was my birthday or something, and that everyone wanted me to feel special. Don't they know I *hate* birthdays?!

Of course the flags were not there for me, they were to celebrate the arrival of President Bush (senior) to Prague: the first U.S. president ever to visit Czechoslovakia. And, we now know, the last — since Czechoslovakia is no more.

Wilson had close ties to Masaryk and the founding of the first republic in 1918, but he'd never been able to visit. And of course during the Nazi and Communist eras, American presidents were not exactly welcome. So it's an understatement to say that President Bush's historic visit on this historic anniversary had many subplots behind it: He needed to stand in Wilson's place, taking thanks for supporting this nation in its infancy. He needed to stand in Roosevelt's place, taking large credit for freeing them of Nazi rule (Yalta kindly forgotten). He needed to stand for two generations of Cold Warriors, who had continually stood up to the Russians and preserved in at least *part* of Europe reasons to hope. But perhaps the biggest shoes of all that Bush had to fill that day were his predecessor Reagan's: the first Cold War president to dare envisage a Prague unbeholden to Moscow, and the first to try to make that too-good-to-be-true dream a reality.

Czechs and Slovaks came to Prague in droves on November 17, 1990 primarily to celebrate themselves. But also in part to say thanks to Reagan for believing in them, and thinking that their freedom really mattered.*

At least an hour before my president was due to speak, Pavla and I made our way toward Wenceslas Square to hear him. That huge expanse was already so full that we were lucky to find a spot to stand just barely within sight of the podium. A ten-foot-wide bullet-proof cage stood empty in front of the National Museum, probably 400 yards away. We didn't dare leave our spot in search of a better one and risk failure, since at least a quarter-million souls had taken root between us and that distant podium.

I looked around at the hundreds of people in my immediate vicinity and, though I'm no fashion buff, studied their clothing. Although their faces bore new, happier expressions of freedom, their bodies still bore the depressing and dull utilitarian clothes of Communism. There was a disconnect there, to be sure: it was as if they had shown up for a wedding dressed in prison fatigues. Their sartorial dullness even more striking since they were waving little sticks with a bright *red-white-and-blue*.

Bush was very late for our engagement, hamming it up I'm sure with Dubček, Havel, and other dignitaries and having one hell of a birthday party somewhere in the parliament building.

---

* Bush of course thought his former boss was a wacky old fool afflicted with some "weird vision thing," so I wonder how this Czechoslovak appreciation for the old nut made him feel. That nagging aspect of the day's festivities aside, I suspect Bush likes birthdays more than I do, and didn't mind the flags at all.

With lots of time to kill, I studied the empty glass cage so far away; and recalled that a Czech friend in Brno, who had been in the military, had told me that he worried about Bush's safety in Prague. Not so much concerned about Bush personally, but more fearing the embarrassment his national pride would suffer if my president were assassinated here, on Czech soil. My friend seemed to take this possibility very seriously. He told me that Iraqi commandos had been training on the outskirts of Prague in 1989, and he was concerned that they might have slipped back into the country. He mentioned that Semtex (the plastic explosive used to bring down Pan Am flight 103) was manufactured in Czechoslovakia – as if that well-known fact now had some important bearing on my president's safety. He seemed to know all sorts of things, only a fraction of which he felt comfortable telling me.

With these strange thoughts of assassination in mind, I began to study my surroundings. And I noticed perched atop every building around the square, at 75-yard intervals, pairs of men. One of these men lifted a scoped rifle into my view for half a second — though the rest were more discreet and kept theirs down out of sight. I wondered what country these dozen or so sniper teams could have come from. I realized they couldn't *possibly* all be American Secret Service. Which led me to the more incredible realization that East-bloc snipers, trained in marksmanship and Communist ideology to the highest standards imaginable, would soon have a clear shot at the American president. More incredibly, I realized that both Havel *and* the U.S. State Department had complete faith in these men! They knew that these elite Czech and Slovak soldiers could not only be trusted to refrain from shooting the leader they had been trained to hate just 12 months prior, but they could also be trusted to take out, in an instant, anyone who tried to do an American president harm. It really defies belief.

Bush finally showed up, and finally spoke, but I can't recall a word he said. I just remember those sharp-eyed snipers looking down on half a million people dressed in ridiculous clothing; and waving small American flags.

On the late night bus ride back to Brno, Pavla slowly fell asleep, and her head tilted to rest on my left shoulder. She snored almost imperceptibly with a deep peaceful rhythm I could just barely make out over the buzz of diesel combustion and the drone of tires on asphalt. I noticed in the dim light how fine her hair was, and how good it smelled. I noticed how good it felt to have a pretty girl sleeping on my arm. And I then thought of Pavla, for the first time, as a potential lover. I reached across myself with my free right arm to cradle the back of her sleeping head in my hand and I put my lips on her dry hair. She woke. Then smiled, grasped my left forearm in both hands, snuggled deep into my chest, and fell back asleep.

Such was the beginning of our physical relationship: gone were our days of peaceful thoughtlessness.

Josef and I became such close friends in those first months after we met, that I think it made the formal process of Catholic initiation a bit awkward. Especially since I took it so seriously, and he seemed to feel this was quite an easy task with certain simple rules and procedures.

First of those procedures was baptism of course, which Josef assured me would be unnecessary since I had been baptized as an infant by my grandfather. But my distrust of Grandpa, coupled with my newfound fear of hellfire, drove me to *insist* that Josef baptize me anew. The stakes were far too high. Hellfire is hot, and forever is a *very* long time.

Over a period of two weeks, Josef and I nearly came to blows on the subject of baptism.

The learned Father held his ground — stating that one *cannot* be baptized twice, and that my infant baptism was perfectly valid.

"I don't believe that," I said. "I'm convinced that my grandfather does not believe in the divinity of Christ."

"That wouldn't change a thing," Josef assured me earnestly. *"Anyone* can perform a valid baptism. He only needs to invoke the trinity and have the intention of baptizing the child. His own beliefs don't matter at all."

"I have no *idea* what my grandfather's intentions were," I blasted back. "I think he was just going through the motions and that he considered this a quaint ritual with no meaning. A cute photo-op, sure. But did he *intend* this to be a sanctifying sacrament? No way. Father, I want you to baptize me." Josef pursed his lips and lifted his eyebrows, and seemed to be at a rare loss for words.

I'm sure he enjoyed being my friend much more than being my priest, because I sure was one ornery parishioner.

Finally, Josef relented and told me that the Church, while never allowing a second baptism, *does* permit what it calls a "conditional baptism." (i.e. "just in case this fellow has not been baptized, I hereby do so in the name of the Father, and of the Son, and of the Holy Spirit. And Father, if he *was* baptized already, please confer a special blessing on him today. *Deo gratia.*")

I smiled in my hard-won victory, looked my friend in the eye, and said, "Thank you Josef, that sounds great. Thank you."

Maybe I …. *even I* … could make it into Heaven after all.

All the while I was debating the finer points of Catholic doctrine with my learned new friend, I was fornicating frequently with my beautiful new lover. I certainly did recognize that there was a problem with this arrangement, but I did not see any other way about it. I needed sex, and I needed salvation. Do those two really need to be mutually exclusive? Really? Then I think I got problems.

The strange truth is that during those many months I led three secretly compartmentalized lives — which perhaps overlapped and met somewhere, but I cannot tell you how or where. With Pavla, I was the passionate lover; with Father Josef, the penitent theologian; with my students and colleagues, the learned man of letters. It was this last part that was hardest to play, since I had just fallen in love with books a few years prior and I still had a lot of catching up to do. The other two came to me quite naturally.

Perhaps the most unpleasant fallout from this odd trinitarian life was its effect on Pavla, who could not possibly understand that she was the third wheel I'd have eagerly parted with if only I knew how.

I was addicted to her body. But her simple soul, which found its unfortunate self falling in love with one much more complicated, was of no interest to me whatsoever. If anything, I wanted to avoid that soul and pretend that it was not there at all. Most damnable of all is the fact that I resented my addiction, and held its poor innocent object responsible for my own weakness. Pavla became my unwitting Eve, and I truly hated her for offering me that fruit.

I'm sorry Pavla, please forgive me. It wasn't your fault.

Journal entry from September 19, 1990

All hearts know the truth – though some can't stand to hear it.

I did not let anyone on the faculty, nor virtually anyone really, know that I was converting to Catholicism. My roommate knew, and my lover knew, but I think that was about as far as I let that little secret go. So I know it was pure coincidence that my kind-hearted boss and friend, Professor Sparling, stepped suddenly out of character one day during a hallway conversation and started to spit venom as he launched, unprovoked, into a vitriolic diatribe against all the evils of Catholicism. It was a remarkable display of unabashed prejudice; all the more remarkable because it was coming from one of the most even-tempered and optimistic men I had ever met.

In a weird way I found the unusually passionate and irrational hatred Don displayed that day … beautiful. It was for me yet another example of the most interesting side-effect of the Communist domination of Eastern Europe: the "museum effect." Not only did consumer technologies (e.g. telephones) seem stuck in the '50's, but human minds did too. Don was a living, breathing fossil: a well-educated WASP from the leafy suburbs of Ottawa who'd been frozen in time circa 1960.* He had never learned that Ontario had gone secular in the '70's when drugs, disco, and Derrida had their destructive ways with North America; and that nobody really got worked up over these irrelevancies anymore. That at the University of Toronto the grandchildren of proud Protestants routinely "hook up" with the grandchildren of illiterate Papists — without even knowing the difference! And that as their young bodies commune so naturally, their unformed minds have no concept of the painful divorce that separated their families nearly half a millennia ago; nor the vast gulf that still stands between them. Instead, all these rich divisions have seemingly dissolved away in grunting and sweating and vain shouts at some forgotten witness called *O God*.

---

* Of course one might say that Don would have turned out the same had he been a long-term ex-pat somewhere in the West, and I can't prove otherwise. I can only state my opinion that I really don't think so. I've met North American academics in Western Europe and they are rarely anachronisms. If anything, quite the opposite — they tend to be one step ahead of whatever intellectual curve is on its way across the Atlantic. Which, these days, is not always a nice place to be. I should add that since I wrote these words Don has clarified his own position on these matters and has made a good case for the argument that my interpretations were all wrong. Very likely … they often were.

I'm certainly not going to suggest that I regret the collapse of Communism, but I do feel fortunate that I got to visit the museum before it closed.

THE SACK OF ROME

There they gathered
high on hill
with smoke of something holy
strangely tingling senses.

One, in deep recess,
scented some beauty
known
but never seen.

Such ancient echoes yet found no voice
midst snarl and howl
and struggle o'er the spoils.

Though one did pause with unfelt ache
to look through darkened lights
toward all t'was his
but not.

Then turned again to fill a grave
with all those things
he dared not save.

One day, I asked Don about my friend Petr back in Hodonín, the kind administrator who had relayed to me Don's generous invitation to mingle with other English-speakers in Brno.

"Oh, I don't know what he's up to now. I heard he got fired and replaced by someone who had never joined the Party."

I was neither surprised nor disappointed to learn that my kind friend had signed on with the Communists at some point in his life — that didn't even register with me. I was just sad to learn that he now had to suffer for the seemingly necessary compromises he had made in the past. I'm sad for him still.

We are all sinners, and some of us sin in our desire to do good. Samuel Johnson said that *the road to hell is paved with good intentions*, and it sure is. Many people got mixed up in the evil enterprise of Communism with the best intentions. Milan Kundera was one of these. And though after his falling out with Communism, and its falling out with him, Kundera went on to write some of the best literature of modern times, I don't think he ever got off that road to hell. Maybe he stayed on it on purpose out of guilt; to expiate his sins. Or maybe he stayed on it out of pride. Most likely though I suspect he stayed on it because, like many intellectuals, he could not get his powerful brain around the idea of God's mercy. It's way too big to understand, and smart people are used to understanding things.

My friend Petr was much more humble than Kundera, so I have hope for him. I suspect he joined the Party primarily because he needed to in order to do the work he was born to do. And perhaps because he had just a little bit of faith in that religion's ability to help people. Those noble intentions though were tainted with the knowledge that he had done something to increase his income, his prestige, and his ability to get the best medical care for his family. In the back of his mind, somewhere, he knew that he had sold his soul for thirty shekels.

It's OK, Petr, we've all done that. God still loves you.

Life was pretty good for me in Brno. I had lots of books with lots of free time to read them; I had a rich spiritual life replete with my own spiritual advisor; and I was surrounded by the things I loved most on earth: beautiful music, beautiful architecture, and beautiful women.

One cold morning I boarded a bus with half of the English department, and about fifty students, to head to a "retreat" in the Moravian countryside. We stayed for almost a week in a barracks of sorts, running an intensive immersion class. The students were not supposed to speak Czech at all … not even amongst themselves.

A dozen or so of them worked with Don rehearsing a play, which they performed the final evening. It was a fairly famous play from a quaint past era: a kitschy anti-war piece set in the trenches of World War One.

Of the students: they were all college freshmen or sophomores, and more than half of them were female. I suppose I should mention the well-known fact that feminine beauty is almost commonplace is the Czech lands. I only mention this to make clear the multiple temptations present here: this retreat was not a good place for a randy twenty-four-year-old Catholic wannabe aspiring to celibacy. Or, failing that high standard, at the very least remaining faithful to his newest unloved lover.

After that play and a bottle of wine I had a little co-ed wrestling match with a nineteen-year-old blonde. I had a vague understanding that she was married, and that did not really concern me much.

Grandpa, you and I are not so different. We both grew up in intellectual wildernesses: you on a farm in Iowa; I in the distant suburbs of Hartford. We both, despite this, somehow managed to immerse ourselves in the best that Western Civilization had to offer. And then we both, in our own ways, attempted to swim out of that civilization's powerful undertow.

We both found ourselves driven by natural forces we could neither control nor understand, and spiritual forces of the same mould. Sometimes these two powers worked in concert, sometimes against each other. Sometimes their relationship was not so clear. But both of them were always there, and they were always bigger than we were.

We both were blessed with wives who loved us more than we deserved; and even though they could not understand us.

I am convinced that I am the only one of your descendants who truly understood you. And the only one who truly hated you.

I love you Grandpa. I'm sorry you had to die to hear that.

On that "retreat" I just mentioned, I got to know quite well a fascinating gentleman by the name of Jan Firbas. Mr. Firbas (I would never call him *Jan*) was the oldest member on the faculty, and certainly the most qualified. He was a true linguist. He spoke the Queen's English with more understanding than she, and without even the slightest hint of any accent other than upper-crust British. He spoke at least a dozen other languages as well, including a literary high-German that went out of fashion a decade before anyone had even heard of a semi-literate plebian named *Adolf Hitler.*

Mr. Firbas could tell you things about Sanskrit, and about other ancient Indo-European languages you'd never heard of; and could tell you how those languages shaped the modern ones we speak today.

Though I call him a linguist, he preferred to refer to his own work as "philology" … a distinction I still don't understand. But his peers did, and considered him one of the greatest philologists of all time. Elite professors from all over the world read and respected his works. Which was terribly embarrassing to the Communist authorities, since Mr. Firbas could not even be called "Professor" under their rule. He was not allowed to travel abroad to deliver the lectures foreign universities had asked him to, nor was he allowed to collect the honorary doctorates that they bestowed on him in his absence. He was, in fact, lucky to maintain any position at the university at all.

You see, there was a problem with Mr. Firbas: He was a Christian, and would share that shameful fact with anyone who cared to listen. Were he not world-famous, he would have certainly been fired and forced to sweep the streets. But the international outrage coming from Harvard and Oxford and a dozen other capitals of learning would have been even *more* embarrassing to the authorities, so they decided to keep him on the faculty at a much lower rank than he deserved. It was the lesser of two evils.

Mr. Firbas was not depressed by his lot in the least. On the contrary, he wore his lowly position as a badge of honor, and curious students continually flocked to him to hear what he had to say. They also liked to simply sit in his presence, even if he were not speaking at all, because to do so gave them a sense of inner peace that they couldn't quite explain.

I understand that "Professor" Firbas finally died eight years after I said goodbye to him; and exactly two thousand years after his master said "it is finished" in an ancient language that my learned friend *also* understood.

There cracked a noble heart.

I met another intellectual giant about that same time — but one who is very much still alive. And, alas, much more coy about his religious beliefs than Professor Firbas. His name is Roger Scruton. Born into a working-class family in England during The War, Scruton's powerful and unique mind propelled him to the privileged milieu of Cambridge University in the early '60's. There, as a mere teenager, he frightened that school's aristocratic professors with his vast knowledge and his unorthodox genius.

He soon went on to write about beauty: What it is, why it is, and how we know it when we experience it. He explored the aesthetics of architecture and music in ways nobody had ever done. He wrote what has become the standard short history of modern philosophy; as well as a slew of other books with deliciously outrageous titles like *Sexual Desire: A Moral Philosophy of the Erotic* and *The Classical Vernacular: architectural principles in an age of nihilism.* In his spare time, he wrote novels. Or composed operas. Or went fox hunting (which, back then, he could still do without leaving his beloved homeland). He now writes, among other things, poetic elegies for the England that was.

In the '70's and '80's, when most of his so-called peers were playing *Variations on a Theme by Marx*, Scruton cried out like a voice in the wilderness. That took guts. Perhaps even more guts than what he did next: He taught himself Czech and Polish and then slipped behind the Iron Curtain to meet with blacklisted intellectuals in dark, wet basements. And smuggled their writings out to publish them, under pseudonyms, in the West.

In doing so, he of course fell afoul of the secret police. Not the tall, blue-eyed variety I had encountered but the real thing: stocky brutes of men who belonged in butcher shops and traveled in pairs. One such pair threw him down a flight of stairs, nearly killing him.

While I was teaching in Brno, this colossus returned to visit old friends – this time with no need to fear flying to his death.

I had heard he was around somewhere, but did not know where. When I walked into the faculty break room after one of my classes, there he was, sitting alone. He was somewhat slouched at a long table, and he seemed very tired. Perhaps he *was* tired; or perhaps I caught him grappling with some new insight into 12-tone music. Regardless, as I entered the room he lifted his head and focused his eyes on mine.

There I was, in a small break room, with the undivided attention of one of the most unique and probing minds of the modern age. That's the truth of it. I knew it then and I know it now.

But I was not nervous ... *he's a man, take him for all and all.* I've never been scared of an individual, it's groups that I fear. That's not to say I was anxious to engage him in serious conversation and to make my poor excuse for an education painfully evident. Hardly!

Mirek Pospíšil, Scruton's friend and mine, was also in the room but quietly reading in an armchair. Mirek quickly got up to introduce us with his impeccable British-accented manners.

"'*Brallier,*'" *the* Roger Scruton asked me, "is that English?"

This was of course just an innocent question about my ancestry, and the linguistic origins of a very unusual name. But I took it as more than that. I felt like the great philosopher was probing me about my Marxist grandfather; and I really didn't want to talk about Grandpa right then.

So I flipped back at him, "No, it's American." And then smirked in dull appreciation of my own puerile joke.

Thus ended my only conversation with a man who was, at that time, one of my greatest heroes.

I still have great respect for Scruton, and hope to meet him again someday. But I now find myself even *more* interested in Professor Firbas; whom, alas, I shall never meet again. Or shall I? I don't dare presume so much.

As the weather turned consistently cold, just before the solstice, I began to get a sense that Christmas in the Czech lands is something very special — unlike anything anywhere else. This superlatively musical, mystical, and magnificent people had, for at least 700 years, done things with this sacred holiday that the rest of Europe could only dream of. And there was no way the Communists could take that away from them.

True, for the vast majority of the populace Christ had never risen from the dead. But by God, Christ sure had been born; and by God, the Czechs were going to do something about that.

I'll never forget hearing their carols sung in *Náměstí Svobody*, and wondering if they sounded just as beautiful before freedom came to Freedom Square. I imagined that they sounded even *more* beautiful back then.

Of course I was wrong. It was not until this book was nearly complete, in 2008, that I learned the full import of the carols I had heard in Freedom Square in 1990 … because only in 2008 did I learn that Christmas carols had been banned entirely from public places during the Red Religion's days in the sun. That incredible thought had, even more incredibly, never occurred to me.

So let's go back to 1990, when young Czechs gathered with joy in Freedom Square and sang about baby Jesus. The first such opportunity to come along since long before they had been born. But such things as Christmas traditions are not easily forgotten. They can quite effortlessly skip a generation or two and come right back on clouds of glory when the time is right.

I remember seeing people I knew dressed up in wild costumes: some devils, some saints, some angels, some beasts. Playing out some cosmic morality play they couldn't possibly have understood. Or did they?

Who cares, it is Christmastime, and we are Czechs. Isn't life grand? Music, music, music. Can't you hear the music?! We must be alive — everything is alive! Even the stones, and the worse than senseless things. Everything lives, at least tonight. Sing, sing, sing! Please don't think tonight, just sing. And dance if you'd like, or whatever you like, just remember not to remember and to let yourself go. Sing. Tonight. At least tonight, for God's sake, sing!

After this sublime revelry, Pavla and I went up to the top-floor apartment she shared with about four other girls. It was in a grand old building overlooking Freedom Square. So it was right in the heart of Brno — which is of course right in the heart of Europe.

Somehow five college girls could afford to live right at the center of the universe, though I doubt any of them truly appreciated how special that was. I think it's safe to assume that apartment has very different inhabitants today. If I had the money, I'd buy it myself. Just as someone with the money surely has.

When we walked in, high on the beauty of what we had just seen and heard, we found one of Pavla's roommates sulking on the couch and chewing morosely on garlic cloves. Zdenka was sick, very sick. Though that's not the only reason why she was not outside singing with us.

Many young Czechs in those days were thirsting for religion, and infinitely more open to hearing about it than young people in Western Europe had been for a very long time. It was a unique and fleeting window of opportunity for the proselytizers, and one they had seized on.

As you know, my friend Jarka down in Hodonín was being pursued by demons telling her that her ancestors had gone to hell for calling Sunday *the Sabbath*.

And this unhappy girl on the couch had just fallen in with another bunch telling her that she'd go to hell if she continued celebrating this pagan holiday called Christmas.

Celebrations with un-biblical roots make Jehova very angry of course, and pissing off Jehova is *never* a good idea.

So there Zdenka sat nursing her illness and nibbling on garlic cloves while rehearsing her bitter new theology and rocking herself gently back and forth like a shell-shocked soldier.

I tried hard to cheer her up. "Merry Christmas, Zdenka! *Vánoce!* It's *Vánoce,* you know. *Veselé Vánoce!*

It didn't work at all, I'm sorry to report.

I sincerely hope Zdenka has become a better pagan than she was when I knew her. Ideally, a better Christian too. But for God's sake, at *least* gone back to being a pagan Czech. There are worse things one could be. Really, there are.

A couple of days after I stared down Jehova's newest Witness, a few of my students cornered me in a hallway and asked with broad sincere smiles, "So Mark, are you going to select your Christmas carp this year?!" The glow in their eyes told me this was no joke … that they were speaking of something very dear to their hearts. As perhaps an un-jaded rural American might talk about selecting the perfect evergreen, cutting it down, and dragging it home through the snow.

Their English skills were quite good, but still I had to ask … "Carp? You mean the fish?" While thinking, *Surely not carp. That scaly prehistoric monster that inhabits the muddy shallows of the Connecticut River? The one that rednecks are permitted to shoot with bow and arrows? Because even the most sensitive-hearted liberals in Connecticut's legislature couldn't give a damn about a fish that ugly? Those carp?*

Yes, precisely. Those carp.

No turkey for the Czechs, no roast beef, no ham. No, no, no. Little kids and adults with some kid left in them can barely contain their enthusiasm as they make their December pilgrimage to the market square. Because they know that on that day they will find waiting for them there a portable swimming pool laden with dozens of scaly carp slogging around in murky water.

"I'll take ... THAT ONE!!"

I don't think anyone knows the name of the practical joker who started this tradition a thousand years ago and made a mint by selling the dim-witted fish he had pulled out of a nearby swamp; but now that so much time has passed and so many little *Ježíšek* birthdays are behind us, there's no going back. The Czechs will (I hope) always adore their Christmas *capr,* and will never forget the first time that mommy let them decide who would live; and even better, who would die.

At the end of my first semester as a Catholic professor wannabe and secular fornicator cannothelpbutbe, I decided to fly home and spend Christmas in Connecticut. So I'm sorry to say I did *not* pick out my Christmas carp in 1990. Though I *did* know where to find them just a few miles away from my parents' house.

The family Christmas party was a surreal and confusing experience for me; but perhaps even more so for the poor people who saw this unfamiliar freak show up with a thick full beard and a bizarre obsession with a distant country of no particular importance. It might have been better if I had spared them my company. Especially considering the fact that the other contender for disagreeable intellectual *du soir* was my younger cousin, who had just flown in from his new home in Berkeley, California. Where he had *also* just undergone a conversion experience. Jacob had become a Communist. And he was very anxious to share his new faith with me. For him, this worldview seemed to be a radical revelation, and he (teenager that he was) reveled in its novelty and rebelliousness. I doubt he knew how un-new and un-rebellious this conversion was, since he had in fact merely found his own way to the faith of his grandfather — and mine.

I refrained from shouting at him, *"Hey, man, I'm the rebel! Not only am I the first anti-Communist this family has ever produced, I'm in the process of converting to Catholicism! Whatdaya think about that, Comrade?!"*

I couldn't entirely spoil my cousin's fun by letting him in on the little secret I had discovered in one of Grandpa's books, and thus accuse Jacob of the cardinal sin of teenagedom – familial conformity. But just the same, having just returned from the gray East, I wasn't going to nod politely and let him go easy either.

So I simply said, "Jacob, do you have any idea how many millions of people have been murdered in that name?"

To which he responded earnestly: "You are not talking about true Communism. *True* Communism is peaceful, and beautiful, and it works!"

Yes, another man of faith had come of age in my family.

I flew back to Paris, and found the Czech bus waiting there to take one pseudo-poor American and fifty truly poor Czechs back to the dark side—where our colorful crowns had some semblance of value.

Just a few days later, after breathing Moravia's polluted air again with pleasure, I made a shocking discovery: Homosexual men had lived behind the Iron Curtain. I don't know why this surprised me, but for some reason it did.

I had attracted male attention in many other places before. As I mentioned earlier, in Milan. But also in Paris, New York, and even rural Storrs, Connecticut. As long as they never touched me (which they never did), I had long before 1991 learned to take their interest in me in stride and to accept it as a compliment.

Unfortunately for him, this East Bloc fellow crossed the line none had before. He was lucky he did not end up in the hospital. And I was lucky not to end up in jail.

I returned late one afternoon from one of my solitary hikes in the hills to find that Frank was having a party of sorts in our apartment. The apartment being small, naturally no space was off-limits. A couple of strangers were hanging out in my bedroom – including a chubby fellow reasonably close to my age. Others wandered in and out of my open door carelessly.

Frank's friend and mine, Mike (a sublimely mischievous medical student), came up to me and nudged me while winking in the direction of the chubby guy sitting on the edge of my bed. And then said, "Careful, Mark, that one's *teplý*." I knew that was the Czech word for "warm." And, since the guy did look a bit inebriated, that designation seemed to make sense.

I hung out with these partiers for a while with some discomfort. Not only because I could not speak Czech well enough to get much of anywhere with them, but also because I wanted to change out of my hiking clothes — and there they were hogging up my private space.

I finally said to myself, "What the hell, we're all men here," and started to change anyway. I was just pulling up my fresh clean pants when I felt a large hand grab my left buttock.

I pulled my pants up all the way and then grabbed this forward fellow by his shirt, slammed him hard against the wall, and shouted at him right in his frightened face (the first and only time I ever shouted in Czech), *"Ještě jedenkrát a BOOM! Rozumíš?!"*

I had no idea how to say in Czech "I'll knock your damn head

---

* One more time and BOOM! Understand?!"

off" so a loud capitalized "BOOM" was the best I could come up with on the fly.

Of course the violent force of my attack sent my pants back down to my ankles; which is exactly where they rested while everyone rushed into the room to see what all the commotion was about.

Mike and Frank laughed, and I would have too. But they also looked at me quizzically as if to say, "What the hell's wrong with you man — lighten up!"

I guess Freud would say that I must be a latent homosexual; that I have homoerotic longings suppressed deep within me; that I need to finally let it all out and be at peace with myself.

Yes, that must be what it is … thanks Sigmund. Thanks for everything.

Journal Entry from July 10, 1990

"The intellectual world of my time alienated me intellectually. It was a Babel of false principles and blind cravings, a zoological garden of the mind, and I had no desire to be one of the beasts."

George Santayana: Persons and Places.

In those first months of '91, I continued going to Mass in Brno two or three times per week, and continued having my Sunday soup at the bishop's palace with my best friend, my intellectual confidant, and my priest all rolled into one. I was very eager for Josef to tell me all the fundamental secrets of Catholicism. To condense for me the key things I needed to know before I could be fully admitted into communion with the church of Peter, Augustine, Aquinas, Merton, and Josef. Oh yes, and of Christ.

Josef seemed confused by my desperation, and would quickly

answer my questions with short simple replies before changing the subject back to the errors that Nietzsche had made or to the funny tricks that the Jesuits used to pull on the secret police or to whatever else we had been discussing before I selfishly tried to turn the conversation toward my personal salvation.

He would, however, pause for an unusual moment when I would mention the massive metaphysical conflict I felt between the desires of my flesh and the desires of my soul. That Heaven and Hell themselves seemed to be having a battle with little ol' me — that I was their rag doll. He would pull in his lips and nod sympathetically. Sometimes he would quote famous theologians who had wrestled with this issue. Once, he did that sympathetic nod of his and said, "I know what you mean, Mark. Women are very beautiful, yes, they are. God made them that way."

Yes, He sure did. So right after my meetings with Josef I'd meet Pavla back at my place and screw the Hell out of her.

And then console myself with the delusion that I really loved her; and congratulate myself unconvincingly for remaining faithful to her. *Maybe she's … the one?*

At the university (oh yes, my job) things were getting difficult because I was running out of new material in my "Teaching Smart Kids for Dummies" books. It was kind of scary.

The students clearly found my textbooks boring anyway, and just wanted to spend our classes discussing anything and everything. *As long as we do it in English, and engage this American in conversation, that's OK, right?* I knew that it was really *not* OK, and that my classes were slowly sliding into anarchy. But I didn't really know what to do about it.

Sometimes I'd get into quite a mess when a student would ask me a sincere question that I could not answer properly … and another of the students could. Sometimes this question would be about grammar, sometimes about the origins of a new word. I'd give it my best shot and then hear something like, "Actually, Mark, the Latin is *suchandsuch* but its roots are from the Greek word *thisandthat.*"

Thanks very much Honza, I appreciate your help.

Invariably, the humble student asking me a question was female and the edgy one making a point of proving the teacher to be a fraud was another male. Interesting dynamic, huh? We've come a long way since the days of clubs and loincloths.

HIVER

O beautiful death!
Cold to skin but warm to heart.
Blankets all, serene embrace,
former self but little trace.

My big day had come. I was to be baptized (as I had insisted) and then confirmed as one of Rome's sons. This was preceded, or followed (I can't recall) by a confession — where I was allowed, for as long as I cared, to speak and to spit out all of the vomit within myself and to come clean before God. What a glorious opportunity that is … one Protestants are fond of mocking but one they might feel differently about were they actually to try it. Freedom is a wonderful thing, and so is assurance from another human being (and even better, a purported authority on these matters) that God really does love you and really can forgive *even that*. You cannot pretend that you are something other than what you are when you are standing before God, as of course you always are, and in the Catholic faith there is no need to try. It's all right there. And it's alright.

I cried quiet tears of joy. I knew that I was not cured of my wickedness, and that this was no magic potion. But I *was* assured that I was not alone. Neither in this world nor in the heavens above it. I'd never been so happy in my entire life.

My joy was sadly distracted when Josef handed me a package of goodies to celebrate my accomplishment. One of these was an impossibly long baptismal candle of kitschy colored wax, and another a rosary molded out of greenish-white glow-in-the-dark plastic. I said "thanks" (I hope) but looked down at the rosary thinking, *"Is that really what I think it is? Glow-in-the-dark plastic?! Dude, I can quote St. Augustine in Latin. Do you really think I want one of <u>those?!</u>*

Truly, no magic potion at all.

Speaking of St. Augustine, I should mention that in preparation for my baptism Josef had informed me that, while it is not required, Catholic converts traditionally take an additional name … one of the saints of their choosing. So for a very brief period of my life I actually had four names, which I later pared down to merely two. I was then known, at least to myself, as "Mark Allen Augustine Brallier." I like to keep only the best company.

And I did keep good company in Moravia. Personally, geographically, and intellectually. The last of which is often overrated; the former two sometimes tragically overlooked.

I am overflowing with unfashionable beliefs, and have very little in common with most of my fellow intellectuals who still breathe the air of this earth. Which is one of the reasons that I have avoided their company for the past sixteen years and have associated myself with humbler, better people.

I have lots of good company and many allies among thinkers who have moved beyond this world though, and I appreciate their companionship very much. As if that statement were not enough, here's just one more bit of lunacy to help modern intellectuals write me off entirely: I believe that all places have spirits, and that all people do too.

The spirit of Moravia is one of a complexity and magic that I cannot even begin to describe it in words ... music is a much better medium for the task. If you are interested in learning about the spirit of Moravia, I'd encourage you to listen carefully to Smetana. If you want to dig deeper and hear the *soul* of Moravia, please, keep struggling with Mahler.

The greatest composer of all time grew up in these magical Czech lands, and he loved them with an ache in his heart: born a Jew, he could never really call them his. He was mystified and forever touched by the fairy tales a Czech peasant had told him. He grew up surrounded by the spiritual and earthy music of these peasants, as well as the music of his four languages: Czech, German, Yiddish, and Hebrew.

When he was a teenager, his brother died ... and Gustav became intensely conscious of his own mortality. As a young adult, he converted to Catholicism. Many think he did so insincerely and for the wrong reasons, but he nonetheless seemed deeply touched by its majesty and mystery for the rest of his days. He sometimes felt intense joy; at others intense sorrow. He was a Romantic aesthete at heart, during an age when that outlook was becoming unfashionable. He felt misunderstood by many people, most painfully by the ones he loved.

Sometimes, especially when I think about my long lost Moravia, I feel like Mahler is my best friend.

But when I *lived* in Moravia, I did not understand Mahler at all. I wasn't ready for him yet.

I was mainly into Mozart at the time; but also fed myself generous helpings of Bach, Brahms, Monteverdi, and some Slavic sacred music that perhaps no other American has ever loved.

One night, I took Pavla to Brno's *Janáček Theater* to see a performance of Mozart's *Don Giovanni*. She dressed like the Slovak country girl she was: in a clashing outfit of brown, orange, and beige; and very tall black suede boots with a band of gray fox fur around their exposed tops.

Pavla mentioned that she had never been to the opera before, and as my consort and I entered the hall she smiled innocently and looked around to get her bearings. We sat, and Pavla watched the overture with wide eyes. But as the opera progressed, I noticed her shifting the position of her long legs more and more often.

The performance was less than perfect, but there were some strong voices and the stagework was quite good. It had *my* attention, but not hers. I recall especially the penultimate scene, when Don Giovanni is dragged down to hell for his philandering:

"Non l'avrei giammai creduto!"

The music spun in a devilish twirl, and dancing stagehands swung orange banners with blinding speed on long wooden poles – so quickly you could hear the fiery cloth crackling through the air over the deafening noise of the orchestra. Feeling the terror of this moment, I looked over at Pavla and saw her looking down, folding her program in new and creative ways.

I wanted to shake her by her arms and ask, "What's wrong with you woman?! Can't you feel this? My God, *can't you?!*" But instead I just looked back at the stage at the manufactured terror there, and then reflected on the genuine terror in my own heart. I thought about mortality and the permanence of history … *Einmal ist keinmal.**

Shortly thereafter, Pavla and I took one of our many day-trips to Prague. A city that, for me, more than lived up to its billing as *The Paris of the East.* I love Paris too, but Prague … ah, Prague. I feel fortunate that I never truly lived in Prague, but was able to visit her so often. So I got to know her body and her soul, and to love them both, but never knew her well enough to know why I should hate her.

I recently read that the Czech capital has, since I last saw her in 1992, been destroyed by tourism, opportunism, and vice. But I suspect that the rumors of her death have been exaggerated. Paris is not the same as it was when Hemingway lived there, but we'll always have Paris. And we'll always have Prague. Or maybe I should say *I'll* always have Prague – as long as I don't go back to see first-hand what the obituary writers are talking about. Maybe it's better that way.

On this particular weekend, the weather was glorious. The sun shone its blessings down on the red rooftops and on us. A gentle breeze brought in a fresh steady supply of oxygen from the Bohemian

---

* "Once is nonce," an oft-quoted phrase in The Unbearable Lightness of Being.

forests. Pavla and I walked beside the Vltava River and held hands as if we were truly in love.

As we strode down the quay on the east bank, near Havel's ancestral home, my subconscious registered the loud sound of a horn very nearby. A quick staccato *Honk honk honk Honk honk honk* then broke through my romantic haze and I looked up to see two beady eyes and one broad smile facing me from behind the wheel of a big green Ford. It was Mike, my bunkmate from that cabin in the Bohemian woods so long ago. He was parked in a travel lane, holding up traffic. I quickly released my grip on Pavla, took the few steps required to approach Mike's familiar car, and leaned down to see his green face again from a distance of only four feet. "Hey buddy, I got somethin' for ya!" he boomed as he reached out the passenger side window and passed me a small black object. It was the travel alarm clock that, in my haste to escape death at the hands of a paranoid schizophrenic, I had accidentally left in the cabin.

"Hey, take it easy dude, gotta go!" He then gunned his Ford's powerful engine and slipped back into the city's magical anonymity.

I sometimes wonder if the psychologists he used to "work for" ever tracked him down, or if he's still drifting through the Czech lands creating new pasts, new presents, and new futures. He certainly picked a good place to do that — I really can't think of a better one.

Lest you wonder, let me assure you that many perfectly sane people from the West descended on Czechoslovakia in those days. Eastern Europe was, in fact, *the* place to be in the world at the time, and a parade of famous writers and academics came through on tour.

William Golding was one of those, and just two years before he died he came to Brno and gave a brief lecture in the same hall where I had first met Don Sparling and somehow ended up with my undeserved job. I had never thought much of Golding as a writer, but of course when I read *The Lord of the Flies* at the age of twelve I wasn't much of a reader. I decided to keep an open mind and hoped to figure out what this guy was all about.

He didn't speak for long, and honestly I can recall very little about his lecture other than how ordinary he looked from a distance of eight feet and how sincere he seemed. After his lecture, I stayed to speak with him. I asked him what he read for inspiration and he replied without hesitation, "Shakespeare. There's no need for a writer to read anything else." That struck me as a pretty remarkable thing to say; which is why, though the rest of his lecture is lost to me, that phrase has stuck with me all these years.

I decided as soon as he had finished that simple sentence that my twelve-year-old mind had been unfair to the old man, and that his books surely deserved my attention. Of course, they still haven't gotten any, and they probably never will. I now hear time's winged chariot.

Which really is a shame because what little I know about Golding leads me to believe that he is someone I really *should* be reading.

I suspect that Golding is one the good guys in 20th century literature; and this suspicion is, I think, confirmed by the fact that my quivering Deconstructionist friend from Seattle did not bother to show up for this lecture given by a Nobel Laureate who intended to talk about such ridiculous inanities as human nature and sin.

Journal entry from October 1, 1990

"The operation of The Green Book and its kind is to produce what may be called Men without Chests. It is an outrage that they should be commonly spoken of as Intellectuals. This gives them the chance to say that he who attacks them attacks

Intelligence. It is not so ... It is not excess of thought but defect of fertile and generous emotion that marks them out. Their heads are no bigger than the ordinary: it is the atrophy of the chest beneath that makes them seem so."

C.S. Lewis: <u>The Abolition of Man.</u>

There is quite a lot of talk about literature and literary criticism in this book, and it occurs to me that I have unfairly thrown a few esoteric concepts in here without explaining them at all. I'm sorry, that wasn't very nice of me. Perhaps I was just being lazy, or perhaps I did not really *want* to talk about these things. I did not want to give them validity by actually putting some effort into discussing them. I still do feel that way, but nonetheless in fairness to my reader realize that I must let him/her/it in on the joke that "higher" education in America became in the '80's.* I really wish I could leave you in the dark on these things – you'd be happier for it.

But no, I will speak boldly and go perhaps where no man has gone before. I will tell you that one of the reasons most of today's college graduates are culturally illiterate is because many of the people who earned their PhDs in the humanities at America's best schools in the '60's, and took control of American universities in the '80's, *want* those kids to be illiterate. They want to speak over their heads and allow them to think that literature once called "great" is, in fact, irrelevant. Because that's what *they* think. Every year they come up with more and more arcane ways to prove that literature is meaningless.

These keepers of culture, who have offices overlooking manicured courtyards and who see ivy leaves fluttering in the wind around the periphery of their office windows, have withered souls. If you walked up to one of them and said, "I love great literature," they'd quickly

---

* I of course only speak of what I know – the humanities. I suspect that engineering departments are still getting by just fine.

size you up to determine whether you were just a harmless fool or if you were a dangerous revolutionary who needed to be kept away from impressionable undergraduates.

In the '50's, some astute observers of academia said that the barbarians were at the gates. The truth is, those barbarians now *guard* the gates. And ruthlessly persecute the dwindling remnants of civilization still left behind them. America's "best" schools have become her worst. There are very few literature professors still left in the Ivory Tower who will stand up to defend greatness and beauty. And they are besieged. A battle is being fought on Ivy League ramparts, and the good guys are losing. They've *been* losing for several decades. When aesthetes and traditionalists *are* tolerated it is only because the vandals feel confident in their victory and know that these few remaining dinosaurs will soon become extinct. They feel that they can afford to be magnanimous with the few odd ducks that still remain.

They are much less magnanimous when they encounter an odd duck younger than they. They try to crush it and discredit it. They would kill it if they could.

As you may realize, I have made myself some pretty smart enemies. You probably do *not* realize that I made enemies of them on the first page of this book. If they read any further than that, they just got angrier and angrier. Now they are *really* pissed because I have, in plain English, spoken to the masses ... the people who really should be eating cake in front of a television ... and told them that the emperor has no clothes — and thinks that clothes don't even matter. They fear I'm trying to start a revolution or something. Yes, that's exactly what I'd like to do.

So that's the broad view, now for the more painful (because tedious) job I promised: educating you on some of the specifics I've loosely thrown in here.

Jacques Derrida: A tremendously influential French intellectual who seemed to speak from Olympus after his apotheosis in

1970. His works are very hard to understand and, of course, are not worth all the tremendous effort that has been put into understanding them. There is a fairly new *Derrida for Dummies* book out there for those unhappy souls who still think that their lives cannot be complete until they grasp the fundamental precepts of Deconstructionism. For two decades or so Derrida ruled as the high priest of intellectual vandalism in the West, and he ordained dozens of other men and women without chests who went around stomping on the grave of Western Civilization. They were terrified that this culture was in fact *not* dead and might come bursting back out of the earth at any moment if they were not exceedingly vigilant.

Deconstructionism: A school of thought and quasi-religion founded by Derrida, replete with its own bizarre language and its own lengthy initiation rituals. Millions of erudite words have been written about Deconstructionism, and it will surely be poorly served by the few dozen half-baked words I intend to give it. But it deserves being so poorly served. It is essentially just an extrapolation of Marxist ideas taken to the extreme. Every "text," including of course the Bible, is "deconstructed" to find its true motives. Motives that are presumed to be tied up in materialist power-struggles. Most "texts" were written by men, so this school of thought is particularly attractive to scholars who resent their fathers for feeling that thirty-year-olds with PhDs no longer need Dad's help — thus forcing these poor children to make a living by teaching snot-nosed undergraduates who don't know shit.

And as these erudite sages stand in front of crowds of worthless undergraduates, they can't help but resent patriarchal governments too — for refusing to step to the plate and to subsidize valuable scholarship once all those Dads claimed they'd gone broke doing so all by themselves.

Aesthete: This really should be a four-letter word, since it means an insubordinate miscreant who thinks that such modern "intellectuals" as I have discussed are ephemeral windbags; and that some things truly *are* great and that others truly *are* beautiful and that politics has absolutely nothing to do with it.

Cubist planes
can touch a face
and leave no space
for pleasing pains.

OK, I'm done … moving on. I hope you enjoyed reading the preceding nonsense more than I enjoyed writing it. I'd like, if you don't mind, to get back to talking about Czechoslovakia. Yes, I know, you are relieved. So am I.

But this is another somewhat sad subject: Czecho-Slovakia. Because at some point in the spring of '91 (about the same time I met Golding I think) I began to realize that the country I loved might break in two. Which seemed tragically premature to me – it had hardly had a chance! It was really only twenty-something years old – like me!

"Czechoslovakia" had been born in a glorious moment of genius in 1918, and then experienced a mere twenty years (but *what* a twenty years!) of creative peace and prosperity before the Germans rolled in. And then the Russians rolled in. And then the Russians rolled in *again*. So 1990 was, in many ways, a rediscovery of the promises of 1918 and a second go at 1939.

But some Slovaks saw 1990 as a chance to go their own way. Most prominent among these was a former Communist hack named Mečiar, who was determined to create a new Slovak state which no longer had any ties to Prague – other than perhaps a sparkling new embassy. Mečiar wanted Bratislava to become a national capital. And in 1991 many Slovaks started following his lead.

I was furious about this, and more than a little condescending. My attitude was something like this: "If you morons want to give up association with the smartest and noblest nation in the world, if you no longer want to call the most beautiful city in the world your capital, well then have at it. If you want to trade *Havel*, a once-in-a-lifetime miracle of a man, for some illiterate provincial hack, then just go for it. You deserve exactly what you'll get."

It didn't help any that I knew the Slovaks did have just a *little* bit of experience running an independent "Slovak Republic" – as Hitler's enthusiastic ally.

Hitler knew that he could never trust the Czechs, so after he took over Czechoslovakia in 1939 he imposed draconian measures in the Czech lands and appointed Germans to rule over them with an iron fist. But the Slovaks had much freer hands, and ruled themselves pretty well in line with Hitler's desires. They even volunteered to send their new army into Poland to help the Germans with their adventure there that same year! And then in 1941, the Slovak State, of its own volition, passed anti-Jewish laws; and, in 1942, good Slovak patriots started herding human beings into cattle cars.

All of that ugly history aside, it also didn't help that I happened to be sleeping with a Slovak girl who stood to lose her association with the nation I *truly* loved and respected.

To her credit, Pavla was completely a-political. As we stood one day on a street in Bratislava watching a rowdy crowd demonstrate for independence, she was completely disengaged and indifferent. She knew the fate of her nation was out her hands, and she didn't concern herself with it. Truth is, she didn't even care about it. She only cared about me.

That same day we looked down on a new piece of artwork on an expanse of gray Bratislava concrete. It was a huge, very nicely done painting of a beautiful building with twin golden domes and exquisite stonework. Beside the painting, in angry blood-red letters, these words: TU STÁLA SYNAGOGA! (Here stood the synagogue!) I looked down on those angry words, and was angry too. And I wanted to add below them my own infuriated indictment: TU STÁLO ČESKOSLOVENSKO.

Back in the divine Czech lands, just a week or so before Easter, two of my younger female students came up to me giggling. One blonde, one brunette. (I tend to remember such details.)

They looked at each other proddingly as if to goad the other into speaking to me. *You. No, you! Come on, you! Go!!*

Finally the braver of the two came quite erotically close to me and said, "Mark, do you know about the tradition of boys whipping girls at Easter?"

I suspect I blushed just a bit as I said, very simply, "No, I've never heard of that."

But my mind was spitting out a whole paragraph that went something like this: *"Well, you girls really are quite charming and make a nice pair, but I think you're only eighteen and that's just a little too young for me. Besides, I hate to disappoint you but I've never been into that stuff. I'm more the romantic caressing type. That's not your thing, huh? Well, I understand, but I think we'll just have to agree to disagree and go our own ways, OK? I really do appreciate you coming over to talk to me though ... that was kinda fun, I must admit. Maybe I'll come around to your way of thinking one of these days, but I really doubt it. Just not me. But I wish you well!"*

It turns out there really is such a tradition in the Czech lands, and its history goes way back to the days of pre-Christian paganism. And for that fact, I am glad ... no blaming Christ for *this* one.

Though I assume Western-style feminism has invaded the Czech soul in recent years, in those days this strange ancient tradition seemed to be one that many Czech girls actually looked forward to. And probably still do, even though they've been trained to feel differently.

Masochism will never be fully eradicated from the female soul, just as sadism is a sad part of what it means to be a man. Personally though, my sadism is purely intellectual. Which is probably why sweet and simple girls who want to be whipped, for real, have never been a part of my life.

No, I had no desire to whip anyone. But I *did* feel an itch to watch someone swing a baton and pick up symphonic music just a notch from the *oh-so-close-to-sublime* level practiced in Brno. The

Vienna Philharmonic sang out to me again, and I had to head back down there.

I boarded a train at Brno's *Hlavní nádraží* and within forty-five minutes or so found myself at that familiar little station in Břeclav near the Austrian border and hiked down to the border just like in the olden days. Everything looked just the same as it had when I lived in Hodonín, though I had changed greatly. I was now a confident local ... just one who happened to carry an American passport. I now spoke enough Czech to get by and to make myself understood whenever that really mattered. And I intuitively understood much more Czech than I actually knew, since that language was becoming the background music to my dreams.

When I got to the border crossing, I passed my blue passport to the Czech official there just like in the olden days — so the fellow could decide whether or not to let me out of this fine prison called The East. And just like in the olden days, he looked carefully at the picture and then at the flesh and blood. But *unlike* in the olden days, he did not then hand the passport back. He looked at it again. And then again at me. And then he asked me with a look of concern on his face, *"Proč tak dlouho?"*

Which I understood very well to mean, "Why have you been in the country so long? You don't have a residency permit."

I just smiled back at him innocently pretending I had no idea what he had just asked me and I replied, in English, "Oh, I'm heading to Vienna to hear a really great band that's playing down there."

He furrowed his brow, scratched his head, and looked both at me and my passport again. And then started to walk toward the hut where his supervisor sat.

Oh, this isn't good.

But before he got halfway there he turned around and walked back toward me. I looked at him hopefully as he gave me my passport back and said quietly, *"Tak, dobry."* He then waved his hand to indicate I should keep moving toward the Austrian customs officials waiting for me just one hundred yards down the road.

Though I have not been back behind the curtain for sixteen years, my understanding is that my forgiving friend is now in a different line of work entirely, as are his Austrian counterparts. There is no longer any border crossing facility here at all; just a sign on one side of the road that says *"Wilkommen"* and another on the other side that gives the same friendly message in Czech.

Journal entry from September 22, 1990

On listening to Brahms' Piano Quintet in F Minor:
There's nothing more beautiful than the tragedy of realizing a beauty lost.

THE END OF EUROPE

Oh, pulchritudo!
Late, too late.
Tragedy
Can be its beauty too.
And pain is pleasing
when only pleasing's
left to please.

V. Allegro con fuoco

TOWARD the end of the spring semester of '91, it occurred to me that I would soon be out of work for the summer. What to do? I was getting low on American dollars, so the remaining tickets to the Vienna Philharmonic were becoming numbered. But I could have easily stayed reading and writing in Brno, and worked part-time at Petr Antonín's private language school and been outrageously overpaid with stacks of colorful monopoly money. Or I could have hitchhiked down communist-paved country roads and floated on my back in the Black Sea. Or smelled Baltic breezes. Or climbed the Carpathians. Or visited the Orthodox Cathedral in Bulgaria where Boris Christoff recorded one of my favorite albums.

Instead, I went to Connecticut and painted houses to recharge my American bank account with dollars. And to show my country to Pavla.

I won't tell you about the 18th century colonial with rotting wooden clapboards and wasp nests. Nor the dreadful mustard contemporary with a mildew problem. But I'd like to tell you a little about my road trip with Pavla.

I bought a rusty old Ford Escort for five hundred dollars from a guy with a hangover and a wicked Massachusetts accent. I then sanded its rust spots away and touched them up with white spray paint from *True Value* — which ran in globs and did not perfectly match the factory finish; but which was close enough for college-kid work.

I drove down to The City and picked Pavla up at JFK. Then brought her into Manhattan to blow her jet-lagged mind. I left the car on West 53rd near MoMA, as I often had in years prior. I knew I'd get a parking ticket, but I also knew that nobody would track me down when I did not bother to pay it.

We took the subway down to the financial district, and an elevator up to the roof of the World Trade Center. We looked out over this weird and wonderful loveable and hate-able thing called New York, and I put my arm around her shoulder as if to tell her this was mine. A strong Atlantic breeze pushed its way up the Hudson and made Pavla's long hair slap my forearm and tickle my nostrils. And as I rubbed that tickle off my face with my one free hand I found myself there, atop the tallest structure that I knew, being interrogated by a voice that only I could hear: *"Mark, why are you here? And why with her? Einmal ist keinmal, n'est-ce pas? Have you forgotten?"*

We spent the night in a cheap New Jersey motel and heard the whore next door pretend that she was enjoying herself and we heard her call her sour John "honey" at least four times. And for the first time in my life I found myself incapable of penetrating the beautiful, naked, and willing body in my bed.

In the morning I loaded our bags into the Escort's little trunk, put the car in gear and let it move us toward the Turnpike. We headed down 95 past every single one of those infamous exits, including the one that would have led me to my forgotten birthplace and the other that would have taken me toward the Pennsylvania farmland where my great-great-great-great-grandfather first learned to speak English and where he first tried, unsuccessfully, to teach his neighbors how to spell and pronounce the name his dead father had left him with.

We crossed America's Iron Curtain into States that long to be something other than United. But which, by force of arms, had been subjugated some five and six-score years prior; and we kept moving desperately toward the safety of that flat senile peninsula called Florida … where such dark memories do not linger.

We entered their little home to huge hugs and welcomes. "Well *helloooo* there!" was one of my grandfather's favorite phrases, and I think he brought it out twice. Pavla was pleased, though a little embarrassed, to find herself the object of such unbridled affection and enthusiasm. She smiled like a shy eight-year-old who'd just been told for the first time that she's really special. She couldn't know that my grandparents were like that with everybody.

I left the poor girl alone to go to the bathroom, and winding my way through the book-strewn living room I noticed a copy of *The Catholic Worker* on a coffee table. This is an obscure journal in most circles, but I knew it well. It's exactly the sort of thing I had been warning Father Josef about when I told him he should consider leaving the Jesuits. It is, as bizarre as this sounds, the official journal of Catholic Marxism. And I felt certain that my grandfather was *not* a closet Catholic. That I had not discovered some undisclosed connection between us.

We all sat down around their little kitchen table, and Grandma asked Pavla about her parents. Not the prying sorts of questions one often associates with these encounters, but just genuine interest. Nonetheless, Pavla's perfectly good English suddenly became strained and difficult, and she answered my grandmother mostly in smiles and nods.

To rescue my lover from her evident discomfort, I started to talk about Czechoslovakia a bit, and pulled a cheap white plastic button out of my pocket. It had a red heart in the middle, and Czech words spinning around its periphery. I first read them to my grandfather in Czech; proud to show him I could do so. I then translated: *"Truth and Love will triumph over Lies and Hate."* I finally added (with an ill-disguised tone of vindication) "That was sort of the anthem of the Velvet Revolution."

I'll never forget, though I have finally forgiven, my grandfather's reply: "That's wonderful Mark. I just hope they can keep some of the good things about Communism."

I wanted to jump up from the table, grab him by the collar, and shout in his kind gentle face, "Just what the fuck is a 'good thing about Communism?!' And how dare you say that in front of my girlfriend! She was born, and grew up, under your beloved Stalinism!

The church her grandparents used to go to now lies pancaked under a Party Headquarters! Pavla's never sat through a church service in her entire life — do you even give a tiny little shit about that, 'Reverend?'"

Of course instead I said nothing at all, and gratefully allowed Grandma to change the subject back to Pavla's parentage.

I must suspect that Grandpa, who always pretended not to notice unpleasant subtleties, had some sense of what his reply had done to me. Because about ten minutes later he said, out of the blue, "Mark, I don't think you can ever understand how terribly poor your grandmother and I were growing up during the Depression."

There was a little less anger in my heart at that moment, but I still could not bring myself to say anything close to what I was thinking: *Don't pretend that's some sort of an excuse. Or that you are now magically absolved from the sin of befriending the devil. It's not, and you're not. But I'm not telling you anything you don't already know when you look in the mirror, am I?*

REQUIEM

Resonance sublime, thrusted from vault
to pew and back again
tumbling rushing bouncing
An essence sucking silence.

Silent ears for which this sounds
had heard before and half-surmised.
Wretched squeezing hearts
Bow and bleed in bloody blackness.

Howls of What Where Why Who
Screamed silently 'tween clasped hands.

Silent ears that yet may see
Light and dark, mist.
Cold stone on half-warm soles,
The remnant left to sing.

From my grandparent's place on the Gulf coast of that thoughtless peninsula, we headed east toward the Atlantic and my brother's apartment near Daytona Beach. We captured and played with a little green lizard that I found on a plant near his front door until it bit us to say *that's more than enough thank you very much* and we let it go. My brother offered to give me a free haircut with his new electric shears and I said *ok* and wound up looking like I had just been sent to the gulag again. I said *thanks bro* and then headed north on 95.

I took in a deep breath of harmless Florida air and tried to hold that breath as Pavla and I crossed into Georgia, back into the heart of darkness. We continued northward as fast as I dared until we got to places that almost know what winter means and I started to breathe again.

When we pulled into downtown D.C., which was very familiar to me, I saw it with new eyes. The grand Greco-Roman architecture took on a fresh sheen, and represented something new. This was the capital of the free world: the place where men, for fifty years, had struggled with the logistics of containing Communism. And despite its corruption, its drunkenness, its vanity, its silly games, and its inherent stupidity, Washington had succeeded against all odds. It had prevented Paris from falling, like Prague, into the grips of Stalin and his successors.

But why?

In the East Bloc, true freedom thrived: the freedom to be imprisoned; to be impoverished; to be powerless. The freedom to think; to work out one's relationship to God and to self.

It's easy to discern eternity from a gray prison cell from which you can see nothing shiny, and in which your conversations are monitored by guards. God is much more difficult to find when your eyes are attracted to pretty lights and you can say whatever comes to your mind to anyone foolish enough to listen.

Paris has no Václav Havel, and probably never will. Her intellectuals waste their long days in freedom, masturbating before each other to the rhythms of their own narcissistic applause. One by one these men die, and as they turn to dust the millions of words they assembled in their lifetimes do too.

The French mind never knew true freedom during the Cold War, though it might have had the United States not kept the Iron Curtain from creeping westward. Thanks to Washington's Pentagon, Paris became a lifeless museum of past struggles — trying desperately to invent new ones out of thin air. Trying to live.

She knew she was dying and called eastward, "Please, take me! Take me in your brutal arms!" But the foolish, stubborn Americans stood between Paris and the rapist she lusted for, keeping the would-be lovers apart. She still hasn't forgiven us, and I understand. I'm sorry.

It's no wonder the German occupation of Paris during World War Two still holds such sway on the French imagination. It's the last time Parisians were truly alive; truly free. The last time they could not speak their mind; the last time they had something truly important to say.

In a similar vein, a man is never free until he is imprisoned in marriage. The bachelor likes to *think* he is free, and his friends are all anxious to back each other up in this illusion, but it's a hollow lie.

That's why they are all so hard on the first guy to get engaged. He's cracking their code, and exposing them for frauds. The truth is (and they know it all too well) that they are prisoners of their own whims. Since everything is possible, nothing is possible. They have so much freedom that they have none: they can't find God.

I love the Czechs, and I fear for them. I fear I saw them at their best, and that it's been a downhill slide since then. It's one of the reasons I've never been back.

Dare I take this a step further? Modern Americans are not truly free either. With our shopping malls, 200 TV stations, Internet, and our cherished opinions, we are spinning in our own custom-made prisons. We are getting dizzy, and can't see clearly. We only hear sounds that we ourselves have created. Eternity tries to speak to us, but we have grown deaf to her faint, beautiful whispers.

Does saying something like this hurt book sales? OK Mr. Editor, you have my permission to delete it.

We continued into indubitably Union territory and passed by *En Why See* again from a new angle so Pavla could see its skyscrapers from a distance and burn still more memories into the cells of her brain that her Slovak friends think make her very, very special.

We spent a couple of days with my parents in Connecticut enjoying the glories of free meals, laundry service, American television, and each other's bodies.

We then continued eastward toward Cape Cod, a place that is eternally sanctified in my mind simply because I spent a week there as a child. Childhood is like that. And I try, often unsuccessfully, to *remember* that as I now raise children of my own. I sometimes wonder what will harrow them with fear twenty years from now and what with wonder. I am very sure that I will be eternally responsible for plenty of both. Lord, have mercy on me; and on them.

My most potent memory of that Cape Cod vacation in the early 1970's is the day Grandpa and I stood in a Provincetown parking lot and he suggested that I could, if I wanted, make the ride down to Truro locked in the trunk of his Buick. He had that deep cavern popped open and I peered into its musty gray space and saw the spare tire in there and tried to figure out if Grandpa was serious. Then, assuming that he was, I tried carefully to decide if I should take him up on his amazing offer or if I should pretend that I wasn't interested.

I honestly cannot remember whether I did or did not make that dark ride back there. If I did not climb in, I imagined that sealed trunk's claustrophobic terror so completely that I might as well have experienced it for real. Childhood is like that too.

Pavla and I found a campground mid-Cape inhabited by a bizarre and frightening mix of lower-middle-class families and solitary men. I set up my Czech tent and then we drove all the way up to Provincetown, since one can drive no further. We sat on the windy dunes in our bathing suits with no intention whatsoever of getting ourselves wet in the waves. We smelled the salt air and watched Atlantic terns pirouette in the wind for only a minute before Pavla reached up the leg of my swimming trunks, toward the elastic mesh that contained me. I smiled and closed my eyes, keeping them only slightly open to remain conscious of my surroundings.

As I looked around through my squint I noticed in the dry sand around us very fine little plants that I recognized quite well. I said, "This is wonderful dear, really, but let's remove to another spot. There's Poison Ivy all around us." Of course she had no idea what those two words mean when they are put together like that.

We actually left Provincetown entirely, and headed back to the campground to enjoy a mid-afternoon repose in my tent. The last such repose we would enjoy before the Poison Ivy oils on Pavla's hand had their angry way with me.

We left the Cape after a couple of painful days and headed west to Sturbridge where my frustration continued. I showed Pavla what American life looked like in its distant past. Which is of course a ridiculous thing to do with a European: they have very different perspectives on time than we amnesic upstarts.

Since we were in that neck of the woods anyway, we spent the night at my parents' lakeside cottage in Holland — Massachusetts that is. It was not a very memorable night.

The next day, I drove westward on Route 20 toward the earthly homeland of my youth ... the Berkshire Hills. I showed Pavla the little white church where my Grandfather had baptized me, and where he shared his new ways of looking at things with an odd mix of grateful, indifferent, skeptical, and hostile parishioners. I then showed her the parsonage that I once called home and the scary stone cottage where the Jewish guy from New York used to hide from the girls he had duped. I was of course speaking Greek to her, so she had no idea what I was trying to say. I had only half an idea myself.

We left Monterey – Massachusetts that is – and headed down Route 7 along the magical Housatonic River. A place that would later become my temple when the traveling circus that is American Catholicism allowed me to walk away from my European Faith in good conscience (or so I thought) and when a pantheistic obsession with fly-fishing took full root. It's no longer any source of consolation or pride to me, but I was far from the first American literary type to fall under that earthly spell. Oliver Wendell Holmes once said that "there is no Tonic like the Housatonic," and I once felt that way too. But I've grown up some since then.

Journal entry from October 11, 1990

"Now it is surely a miserable slavery of the soul to take signs for things, and to be unable to lift the eye of the mind above what is corporeal and created, that it may drink in eternal light ...
I grant, however, that they who make gods of the works of man have sunk lower than they who make gods of the works of God. But the command is that we should love and serve the One God, who is the Maker of all those things, the images of which are worshipped by the heathen either as gods, or as signs and representations of gods."

St. Augustine: City of God.

We parked by the river's limestone banks and got out on that sweltering August day to cool our feet in the slowly flowing water. We did not get very far though before I yelled, "Pavla, stop!!"

There ahead, *mirabile dictu*, sulked a large group of the largest brown trout I had ever seen in my life. They were all in very shallow water close to the riverbank. There were at least a dozen of them, and every single one was truly trophy-sized. You probably don't know this, so I'll clarify: that means more than twenty inches long. I was not yet a *true* fly fisherman, so I did not know why these huge fish were all stacked together like that in such a vulnerable lie. Neither did I know that they were in no mood to eat.

I scrambled up the riverbank back to my beloved Escort, and pulled a cheap fiberglass fly-rod out of the truck. I strung it together by the roadside, forgetting that I had abandoned my lover on the rocks below. I had simply ordered her to stop, mentioned something about huge fish, and then run off on her like a madman.

Once the rod was fully assembled I reached for my box of flies … and then smacked myself hard on the forehead. *Damn!* I could picture exactly where I had left that box – on a rock in Connecticut. I threw the now worthless rod down beside the car and scrambled back down the riverbank. The fish were still there, and so was Pavla. Now what?! The primitive hunter in me (which would later be civilized by the well-researched doctrines of pantheism) could not leave these large fish unmolested. I had to get one of them somehow. Anyhow.

I entered the river fifty feet upstream from the trout (I now know that a downstream entry would have been craftier) and waded out toward the middle of the river. I then walked downstream so that this pod of fish was trapped between me and the riverbank. And then I slowly, carefully, closed the distance.

All the while Pavla stood in the hot sun on that rocky riverbank learning lessons about nature and about me.

I shuffled my feet slowly, and was amazed that these fish seemed completely unaware of my presence — even though I was now only ten feet away and could now see that they truly *were* as big as I thought at first glance. Maybe even bigger.

I then put my arms out wide and charged toward the riverbank. The fish all scrambled away from this fanatical invader, but not nearly as quickly as I would have expected. The misfortunate one who found himself trapped between my feet and the riverbank just swept his fins helplessly as I pounced on his broad back with both hands. I then lifted up his bulk with a smile and a shout, and carried him proudly over to the pretty feminine gatherer I had slept quietly beside just twelve hours prior.

The heat-stressed trout gave up the ghost almost instantly when faced with such overwhelming force. I laid his limp corpse down on the hot rocks, and ran up to the car to grab the tape measure I very occasionally needed when painting houses.

"Twenty-three inches! *Twenty-three!!*" I was of course still speaking Greek, but Pavla smiled and tried her best to share in my mysterious masculine joy.

A couple of years later I would think back on this incident with shame, since brown trout had become the cows of my New Hinduism.

I learned in my catechisms that those poor fish had all been concentrated near a tiny coldwater spring in a desperate effort to get some oxygen and to survive until nightfall, since the river's main body had risen to a temperature that their bodies could not tolerate. Any fool could have killed them. This fool certainly killed many more than the one fish he grabbed, since he chased that blessed congregation out of its cool sanctuary and into the deadly fires of the River Styx.

May Charon have mercy on my heathen soul. I knew not what I did.

VI. Larghetto accelerando

They've taken the human out of the humanities, and the man out of the human.

WHEN I was still an undergraduate, I took a graduate-level class in Shakespeare. You might reasonably assume that we learned a lot about Shakespeare in that class. But if you're one of the initiated, you know that we did not study Shakespeare at all. We were too advanced for that.

Truth is we were all so smart that we had nothing at all to learn from, or about, The Bard. So we learned instead about isms and how to apply those isms to whatever "texts" someone might put in front of us. Marxism and Feminism were the two most common angles, the latter being the most unassailable of all. Other world-views may come and may go, but don't dare question whether texts from the Elizabethan era contain within them the evil thumbprints of gender injustice. *Of course they do!*

That obvious statement aside, the underlying assumption was of course that no text, no matter who had written it, could possibly contain anything of lasting value. Which of course begged the question, "then ... why are we even doing this?" I'm sure there was a good ten-thousand-word answer *to* that question, I just don't know what it was. I was smart enough not to ask.

I also had enough sense to keep my aesthetic sensibilities in check

---

* The irony that the very name of this phallocentric era comes from that of a powerful female ruler is best left unobserved. Irony is ideology's fool.

and to go with the destructive deconstructionist flow, since I felt that getting an "A" in a graduate-level course might make the difference between Yale Law and The Des Moines School of Ambulance Chasing. Of course I was wrong in at least one respect: I did get an A, and I *still* didn't get into Yale.

There were only seven of us in that room. Professor Matt Proser, John Smith, and yours truly represented the oppressor class. The other four were women.

I tried really hard to be a good feminist, and was graciously given at least a *little* credit for effort. But still I fell short.

One night I had to present a report to the class on a piece written by the Marxo-feminist Marilyn French, whom I referred to very consciously as "Ms. French" — assuming Gloria Steinem would approve. Well the times they were a' changin' and Gloria Steinem's monikers no longer cut the mustard. One of my fellow students politely interrupted my presentation and asked, with a smirk, "Mark, why do you call her '*Ms.*' French'?" I did not have a good answer of course, but just looked back at my inquisitor begging sympathy as I thought, *Come on, Steph, you know I'm just an undergrad so cut me some slack ... please?*

Professor Proser was always kind to me though, and never asked me to confess my un-correct sins in public. In fact, sometimes I felt like he and I were in on the same joke. I don't know, I guess it was the way he smiled sometimes. I thought, *You know, this old duffer actually believes in beauty. He just accepts that we need to go through certain motions in order to live the good life. That these days we need to shovel a heavy load of manure if we want the right to enjoy a green pasture. It's worth it.*

I could be all wrong about him, but I felt that in his heart of hearts Matt was a good guy who had fallen in love with Shakespeare sometime around 1935; and then five decades later found himself going through the motions of academic vandalism simply because that's what was expected of him in 1988. He was just a player playing his part.

Well this has all been a long detour away from the period this book is supposed to be covering, and I'm sorry for that. I just wanted to give you a little background on the distinguished gentleman I visited in England in 1991.

Professor Proser and Professor Proser (his wife, whom I'd never met) were on sabbatical in London, and had invited me to spend a few days in the house they were tending while the English professor who owned it was on an American sabbatical of his own. It was a modest brick row house in a clean and quiet working-class neighborhood. I arrived there on a Sunday afternoon just after teatime, and I suspect the rest of the neighborhood was quietly reading *The Sun,* watching football on the telly, or dozing off with a pint as I knocked on the Prosers' wooden door.

They both greeted me with the warm reserve one expects in such unequal intercourse. Mr. Proser then showed me to my room upstairs while his learned white-haired wife prepared tea in the kitchen below. I took a moment to rest on the bed before heading downstairs for what was sure to be an interesting conversation. I was a little nervous about speaking with Mrs. Proser, since Matt and I had a fairly good rapport already but she and I were complete strangers. It surely was awkward for her to host an unknown kid young enough to be her grandson. Or perhaps she was used to that by now?

Once I composed myself well enough to speak half-intelligently, I headed down the stairs. We sat in the cozy parlor, each in our own armchair, at the points of an equilateral triangle. So with the subtlest movement of the head, we could direct our attention to one or the other of our two companions.

Naturally, the pleasantries of talking about misty rain and the ferry ride across the Channel done with, the conversation turned toward Czechoslovakia. And as it did, I noticed Mrs. Proser's face tense up. Her eyebrows lowered a bit and she seemed very focused on my every word, while sharing fewer of her own. My teacher was as easy-going as ever, and kept things moving with lighthearted questions and occasional off-topic diversions like giving me updates on my former classmates. "Oh, by the way, Stephanie just wrote to me … she's going to law school too!"

Mrs. Proser finally piped in and demanded of me angrily, "So how are the Czechs dealing with the new economic reforms?!"

Put off by her strange and sudden aggression, I replied coolly, "Oh, it's not all easy of course but most of them are being very mature about it."

The old lady had absolutely nothing to say in response to such a vile provocation, so after five seconds of awkward silence my former teacher quietly offered me this: "You know, Mark, many of our colleagues at UConn think that Gorbachev is a traitor to *The Cause*." His wife nodded reflexively, remained silent, and stared at me intently.

The man of the house then offered me a kind half-smile, and the subtlest of winks.

Yes, we really were in on the same joke — one my Czech friends might not have found very funny.

My cheery report to Comrade Proser was a half-truth at best, since it really only applied to the young and educated circles that I traveled in. Many older Czechs, of Mrs. Proser's generation, were grumbling quite frequently about the harsh realities of transition to a market economy. And of that fact I was very well aware. So aware in fact, that just weeks before visiting the Prosers I had submitted the following article to a magazine in Prague — after my lovely office-mate spent many hours carefully translating it into Czech for me.

How I See Czechoslovakia

There has been much talk these days, in my opinion too

much talk, about the poor economic situation in which the Communist Party has left Czechoslovakia. I think it is important to realize that the Party never intended to impoverish your country – this came as an inevitable side-effect of its hateful ideology.

Yet more important to realize that poverty is not the worst thing the Party has left you with. It has left you with a legacy of hateful and materialist thinking. How often have I heard people whisper suspiciously about their neighbor's new car, satellite dish, or what have you. More disturbing is the often-heard grumble, "Did you see how much refrigerators cost today?! Things were much better under the Communists." In my anger I am tempted to say that these people deserve exactly what they will get. But it's not so simple. If the Communists gain more power in the next election it will hurt everybody – not only the hateful and immature people who put them there.

There are yet others who hate the Communists for impoverishing the country and thus denying them the right to drive a BMW. These people, though professedly anti-Communist, have nonetheless been seriously influenced, one might say damaged, by Communist ideology. Communism is a complicated intellectual stance that is founded upon the belief that only material things matter. But, as others have pointed out before me, a high-brow materialist philosophy quickly degenerates into primitive selfishness: "I want!" Greatly simplified, the Party said that, since only material things matter, we must try to achieve material equality. Many people have accepted the premise and come to a different conclusion: "Since only material things matter, I want more of them." This kind of selfish and short-sighted thinking (which, incidentally, has a very prevalent and damaging influence in the West) is nothing to found a stable democracy upon. Materialist thinking, in <u>all</u> its forms, is in my opinion a very serious threat to the future of democracy in Czechoslovakia.

So, this is how I see things. I'm sorry I have not spoken about how much I love this country or how much I enjoy living here – that must wait for another article.

Looking things over, we inevitably come to Lenin's question, "What is to be done?" In my view the answer is to be found in those sources of patient, traditional wisdom that our age has largely rejected. Look to Masaryk – there is a world of wealth to be found there. You might even (as Masaryk would suggest) see what is happening in your local church. Above all, be patient, be hopeful, and look for things to love, not to hate. I wish you all the best.

The paternalistic piety of this piece is embarrassing to me now, but then so is much of the folly this book contains. It all just is what it is … I cannot not start re-writing myself now.

Fortunately, the magazine never ran my rant, so the urbane Czechs who subscribed to it were spared my revolutionary insights into their characters and their problems.

Since I have already presumed myself worthy of speaking on these matters, I will take it even further. And I will even be brash enough to look into the future.

But first, a look back:

In Communist Czechoslovakia, where nearly every aspect of daily life was influenced by a paranoid system which sought to mold each individual's inner self in its own image, a strange thing happened: the system usually succeeded. Hardly a single soul was left completely untouched by the compromises of Communist life.

This is a phenomenon Václav Havel talked about often and at length while he was president of my beloved second homeland. Havel felt that even he, the individual who had gone to prison for speaking against totalitarian oppression, had been one of its co-conspirators. That he, and everyone else in the country, had some apologizing to do. And incredibly, he was pretty much right. He certainly overstates the case, especially in his own instance, but he does so to his credit.

Shakespeare spoke about corruption's fecundity: how it breeds and multiplies itself naturally. This was nowhere clearer than in the East. Human minds, human characters, and human behaviors were nearly all corrupted by that system at every level of society. As levels of achievement increased (be that in sports, industry, farming, the arts, or just about anything) so did the required level of moral compromise.

Compromise was a part of daily life in the East. Some people compromised reluctantly, some eagerly. Only a handful made a serious effort to consistently remain true to their better selves; and most of those happy few woke up one day in jail or an insane asylum. A happier few did not wake up at all.

I crossed paths with many guilty consciences in 1990 and 1991, and those were all good people. I crossed paths, unfortunately, with even more atrophied consciences: people who had grown so accustomed to choosing expedience over justice that they no longer knew the difference. Or to speak more truthfully I think, people who had suppressed their own knowledge of right and wrong so often (and done so with such a large and powerful cheering section) that this all-important knowledge lay dormant, deep within them, in a dark corner of their forgotten souls.

In America there has been for several generations a certain class of man I'd like to paint. This is the man who, as a child, always wanted to be on the winning team, and did everything he could to achieve that blessed state. He wasn't concerned with *anything* but winning. When a coach would try to console him with talk of "a game well played" he'd roll his eyes because the coach was obviously a moron.

He didn't usually cheat – but only because he knew he'd get caught. He learned the rules carefully — so he could bend them to his advantage at every turn. It's quite obvious that without well-thought-out and well-enforced rules he would have become an abject monster.

He got through school with the same mindset — very concerned about grades but not whatsoever with the learning they represented. He studied only because he could not find a better way to win.

When he got into the corporate world he played that game pretty well too. He smiled when he needed to, "kept his nose clean", and rose to a certain level of financial success. For several decades, he provided well for his family, never got caught cheating on his wife, and finally died a "success." You can now see his name on a bleacher at his alma mater's football stadium. Even sit on it if you like!

Well in the East the same sort of boys and the same sort of men existed. But the rules were very different there. Cheating was the norm, old-fashioned rules were for sissies, and honest bookworms were thrown in prison. Now *this* was a place an ambitious boy could do some damage! These men, even though they had bourgeois grandparents who deserved to have been liquidated before they bred, joined the Communist Party. It was, of course, the winning team. And the only means to provide well for your family, to manage to afford a mistress, and to get your name on a plaque somewhere.

In 1990, when I met these guys, they were studying the rules of corporate capitalism with a vengeance. They were determined to win at the new game too, and of course they have succeeded. I know the country has too, but that incontrovertible truth is one I sometimes find hard to swallow when I remember who's making billions of dollars over there and who still, to a large extent, is calling the shots.

Now for my bold look ahead at the brave new world to come:

I believe that the greatest challenge the former East Bloc nations will face for the next fifty years will be allowing morality and entrepreneurial ambition to cohabitate peacefully in the same breast. The Russians will of course never get there, but I think the more noble Czechs just might. That is, *if* the Russians don't render that impossible. That's a much bigger *if* than most people realize.

OK, since I'm not really keen on ingesting radioactive materials, I think we probably should get back to irrelevancies and talk about things that don't matter. Like literature maybe? Yes, let's.

Journal entry from September 22, 1990

I received news from America that "Deconstructionism is dead!" This seems redundant to me, as all "isms" are stillborn.

During the fall semester of '91, I taught a course on Shakespeare for final-year students in Masaryk University's English Department. It was of course an optional elective, and only four signed up. All four were women just a little younger than me; and all four were, by the terms I would have judged them only a year prior, imminently beddable. But this thought never occurred to me once. I really was there for the sole purpose of engaging their minds and helping to shape their souls with the greatest literature ever written. I took this task to heart, and very seriously.

I just now, seventeen years later, looked over the syllabus I had prepared for those poor girls, and I feel just a little sorry for making them work so hard. But also amazed that three of them kept up with me eagerly, and that one of those three (the most attractive of the bunch) really got it. She knew why I was driving them so hard, and she felt it was worth it. She understood that "Shakespeare" was more than a famous name — that there were mind-boggling insights into human character to be gleaned, and clean aesthetic pleasures that can be compared to no other. It was truly a joy teaching her and sharing my non-corporal passions with her, while I preserved the other sort wholly for Pavla.

In one semester I somehow gave these girls an overview of The Bard's entire opus, and pushed them through three plays in great depth: *Hamlet, King Lear,* and *Henry V.* On top of that, I gave them a basic understanding of how all the history plays fit together. And even managed to expose them to the literary criticism of Johnson, Bradley, Harbage, Wilson, and Eliot. All of whom were very much out of fashion in the American Academy; but whom I was completely free to extol, here in The East, without concern that the thought police would come knocking on my office door.

It occurs to me now not only that I should have covered less material in one mere semester, but that I probably should have included one of the comedies — especially since most readers without penises seem to prefer those for some reason. But this was *my* class dammit! None of them thought to complain.

I gave them short quizzes every week to make sure they were keeping up with me and actually doing their homework. Only one of them was not. I gave them several lengthy writing assignments too. I was a brutal taskmaster.

The one of the four who blew me off completely, and really should have failed the course, had my sympathy even then. She very obviously plagiarized her papers from Marxist scholars much smarter than she, but I did not have the heart to call her on it. I just gave her the Czech equivalent of a "C" and pretended that I hadn't noticed.

Other than this Shakespeare class, my third semester of teaching was a complete disaster. My "conversation" classes descended quite fully into the abyss of nihilistic anarchy. I spent virtually no time preparing for these sessions in which I was charged with polishing the English skills of at least fifty highly intelligent individuals. OK, I should not overstate the case – they were not all geniuses. But they were no dummies either. And they certainly deserved better than this dummy was giving them.

I permitted my students to take control of their direction – because I really couldn't care less. The students seemed quite pleased that I had finally thrown out the textbooks I'd been trying to push them through, which were really too simple for them anyway. They also seemed to enjoy having more opportunities to push the envelope of propriety with me, and often tried out esoteric English swears they had picked up somewhere or other.

The conversations sometimes took bawdy turns that frightened me. Especially since I was pretty sure these kids knew that I had, a year prior, rolled in the Czech hay with a couple of their own.

I feared that as the barriers of politeness fell, eventually one of them was going to ask my opinion of Czech pussy ... just to try out yet another vulgar word and to see if I'd blush. Perhaps they *would* have asked that question if one of those pussies were not also present, and trying to pretend that she did not know me any better than they did. Thankfully her fellow students were kind enough to her, and to me, never to take things quite that far.

Though I spent virtually no time trying to maintain some useful order in these large classes, I spent an *outrageous* amount of time every week preparing to turn four twenty-one-year-old Czechs into world-class Shakespeare scholars. Now *this* was important!

I resolved about that time to abandon forever my idea of going to law school, and decided instead to take on the American academy and get a PhD. It was a thought that truly terrified me, since I knew that it meant fighting tooth-and-nail, every day, with men and women without chests who will clench their teeth and shake when they look at me and will do anything they can to destroy me. Because I represent everything that is wrong with the world. Because I want to restore literature to a place of respect. Because I want to pick up the dust that these so-called scholars have left in their wake and re-assemble it and re-package it and help young people fall in love with greatness and mystery. Because I want to pretend that there is some sort of mystical continuity in the human experience, and that the Greeks and the Romans were often onto things worthy of our attention. Because I think that the fundamentals of the human condition really haven't changed since Aristotle's day, despite all the "advances" we have made since, and thanks to, the French Revolution. Because I don't give any credence whatsoever to the articles of faith that the faithless live by.

Be brave, Mark, you can do it. If not you ... who?

Journal entry from October 11, 1991

He sees no difference between Paradise Lost and Pravda – yet seems more inclined to believe the latter.

There are many intellectual questions raised in this book of which most people have only the vaguest sense. God has blessed them not to understand these things as well as I do. Understanding them is not a thing to rejoice at.

Our nation's soul is sick, even unto death, and everybody knows it. Many people sense it intuitively, but cannot even begin to put it into words. They can sometimes critique the things and the values they see on television, but they don't really understand where these things are coming from.

Philosophy, like water, trickles down; and television is soaked in this water. Being, as it is, beneath everything.

Every single idea in the world has philosophical and theological implications. The cutest little catch-phrase that you might hear on Oprah has lofty intellectual underpinnings which may, or may not, be sound. Or it may have a seed of truth in it that has been corrupted by soaking in bile; or compromised by being forced to conform to some other belief with which it is not compatible. Much of what you hear though is just untrue, plain and simple.

Now many people reading this are surely reacting, "Hey, you can't say that! Everyone's entitled to their own opinion!" And what you have just done, perhaps unknowingly, is recite one of the most unassailable articles of faith in the religion of modernism — the belief that there is no such thing as objective truth, and that all values are relative. But it's a lie, and you know it. If you don't believe me, take it to the extremes and come up with some examples that work for you. Is A just as good as B? Is C just as *true* as D? Of course not. You have to be very intelligent to truly believe something so foolish. I hope you are not that smart. I once was; but God, in His mercy, taught me to be a fool.

Relativism is just one of the illnesses of our age. There are many others I'd rather not talk about right now.

People are clearly thirsting for some spiritual direction, and some lasting truth. But the saddest thing is watching them try to conform whatever truths they glean to the fashionable falsehoods they still cling to. It's an impossible task. They do not realize what they must throw away in order to attain the peace they seek. They must throw away the entire bible of false beliefs that they have been living by for decades. And they must – absolutely must – disconnect their televisions; since that box continually reinforces these destructive beliefs in subtle and not-so-subtle ways. They will never escape their prisons if they refuse to take this radically liberating step.

We humans have lived for thousands of years … and have lived. Yes, it is painful sometimes (thanks mostly to our own sinful natures), but we all have choices to make. I would encourage you to choose life.

The Appian Way

Pacing through the breaths of must
I listen to some stones.
Stones of stone forever crushed
sound soft on softer bones.

A learned Roman walked this way
with stoic pagan gait.
Reflecting on his world once great
which late, had gone astray.

Words but words
when thoughts have turned
yet silent stones still speak.

Of seeming sameness
was, was not
cannot
should never be.

Sometime around Thanksgiving, Pavla and I spent a weekend in Budapest. Of course there is no such holiday as "Thanksgiving" in Europe … I just use it as shorthand for that brief indecisive season between fall and winter.

One of my smartest students in Brno had somehow found herself an American boyfriend living in Budapest; and this guy had, through her, invited me to use his apartment while he was out of town. I had never met him, and still have not. Though I'd love to fix that one of these days.

Armed with little more than an antique set of skeleton keys and an address written hastily on an envelope, Pavla and I boarded a train headed for another East Bloc nation.

The Hungarians have at least a few things in common with the Czechs. Of course both of them prepared during the Cold War to fight the "imperialist" forces based in neighboring Austria. But they both also bristled under Communist domination. And the Hungarians, like the Czechs, *also* had a serious go at throwing off the Red yoke. They actually beat the Czechs to that distinction by more than a decade, rising up in 1956 with whatever weapons they could get their hands on. And, like the Czechs would twelve years later, discovered the constancy of Russian resolution and the frustrating futility of banging pieces of wood against tanks.

Though it ended in defeat of course, that famous '56 uprising is one of the finest chapters in modern Hungarian history. One of very few fine chapters really. Because unfortunately the Hungarians have even *more* in common with the Slovaks. Like the Slovaks, the Hungarians also allied themselves with Germany during World War Two, and almost out-Hitlered Hitler as they took full advantage of this brief window of opportunity to rid Hungary once and for all of the root of all its problems … the four hundred thousand Jews who once called this land home.

Truth be told, I don't like Hungary much. I *would* very much like to encourage people to go there though – to take some of the pressure off of places I like better.

A few years ago I read a quasi-autobiographical novel written by a Harvard-educated kid from Minnesota, of about my age, who taught English in Budapest and fornicated with his students while I was doing the same in Brno. The book is primarily about Budapest and the obnoxious ex-pat community there – of which the author was evidently a part. Personally, I avoided such communities very carefully wherever I went.

His book is, of course, entitled *Prague*. Huh? Well, two points: First, nobody would buy a book called *Budapest,* would they? Second, one of the weaker themes in the novel is a wistful melancholy which settles on the American ex-pats in Budapest when they realize that they *should* have settled in Prague. Of course they just would have hung out with drunk and obnoxiously self-important brats there, too, so what difference would it have made? That point aside, these brats were of course right. Prague is Prague and Budapest is … well, Budapest. But personally I'm glad that at least *some* of these shallow ex-pats staggered around the no-mans-land of Buda-Pest. By the summer of '91 the best parts of Prague were already infested with them.

It was not until I'd been wandering around the Hungarian capital for several hours that I first learned that it is really two cites: Buda, and Pest. If you didn't know that already, don't feel bad. And if you *did* know that, don't pat yourself on the back too hard. It's not really all that important; and we are not playing *Jeopardy* right now.

When Pavla and I finally figured out how to read Hungarian street signs and found our way to the apartment, we were both exhausted. We struggled up a narrow ill-painted hallway past a suspicious stare or two, found on a well-worn door something which vaguely resembled the numeral on my envelope, and gave the old key a try.

We were in! I collapsed on the bed beside Pavla and thought about nothing at all for a blessed ten minutes or so. I then got up to get my new bearings, and studied the jam-packed white bookshelves. A bit of history, a bit of philosophy, a ton of literature, and a framed color picture of some little red-headed kid (whom I assumed to be a nephew or something) decked out proudly in his Cub Scout uniform.

I liked my student's mysterious American boyfriend — a lot. And I feel quite confident that the apartment I borrowed in Budapest was *not* inhabited by the author of *Prague*.

But Arthur, if it that *was* your place, I'm really sorry about your cooktop. I didn't know that I was supposed to remove the cover before turning it on. Actually, I didn't realize that *was* the cover. And I'm sorry I just dissed your book. I'll give it another try before I die — I promise. If you'll forgive me for disfiguring your stove I'll forgive you for duping me with that beautiful title. It's OK, I probably would have done the same thing if I'd been in your shoes. Bummer you can't just hit rewind and make some different choices, huh? I know the feeling.

Finale: *Adagio Misterioso*

IT was cold in Brno and I found myself spending a lot of time alone, riding around town on drafty trams with hard metal and plastic seats.

With my head slightly lowered, I'd watch peripherally the dusty churches and apartment buildings and schools and parks as they passed me by. I'd listen to the Czech lovers behind me whispering consonants to each other and I'd feel the sway of the motion as the whole weight of this weary world weighed heavy on my too too intelligent soul.

I could not read a book; I could not turn my head to look at the familiar sights passing on the movie screen beside me; I could hardly breathe.

What am I? Why am I here? And here?

The tram would pause near the main train station, and I'd lower my head even further so I could not see a place where people were boarding trains that would take them to other countries ... perhaps back to their own?

I'd stay on that antique red tram as it accelerated hard away from the station, trying to gather speed before it needed to climb one of Brno's steepest hills, and I'd finally lift my head to glance up at Petrov's brown cathedral or Špilberk's dusty yellow walls. I'd study the red brick of Brno's oldest Protestant church more carefully, and wonder about the theological implications of man-made brick versus earth-hewn stone.

I'd think of the university where I'd need to show up the following day with some sort of plan ... or not. I'd think about Professor Firbas and the rest of that blessed faculty, who had suffered so much for so long but who now went about their jobs in peace, unmolested by thought police of any sort. I'd think about a nation that now seemed more free than my own. And I'd remind myself, painfully, that this nation was *not* my own.

I loved Czechoslovakia with all my heart, even though she was not mine and could never be mine. I did not love Pavla with any of my heart, even though she was mine for the asking with all of hers.

So I had to leave them both.

We stood in Brno's polluted bus station for twenty minutes in silence beside a large wheeled box with the word "Paris" pasted high up on its windscreen. We could not speak. What was there to say?

Finally, the driver said it was time to board, and words were forced upon us. I looked Pavla straight in the eyes for the first time in a long while and noticed that those eyes were glistening with moisture in the crepuscular morning light — though her cheeks were blessedly dry. Her chin quivered almost imperceptibly as she spoke just ten words: "Mark, remember that you are responsible for what you do." The first philosophical phrase I had ever heard cross those innocent lips.

Yes Pavla, I remember.

I climbed onto the bus as she stood there all alone on the curb with her Slovak scarf wrapped tight around her neck and a silk handkerchief wrapped tightly around her hands. I sat in a seat where she could see me, though I wanted desperately not to see her. The bus's engine was running and its familiar buzz reminded me unkindly of that night so long ago when Pavla first fell asleep beside me.

Finally, mercifully, the driver put the bus in gear and started to pull me away. I pretended to look back at my lover's body one last time, just for her sake, and lifted a hand limply. Then put it back on my lap, looked down at my knees, and took in a deep breath of the polluted air around me.

As the bus left the station, I could see Peter and Paul's brown cathedral towering over me once again, and Špilberk Castle's yellow walls daring me to climb them. I could see the spire of Josef's church just barely making itself known. I could see Brno's medieval grandeur competing with her modernistic future.

The bus started to gather speed and to take a long sweeping corner toward the freeway and to leave the sights and smells of Brno behind it.

I closed my eyes since there was no longer anything to see. I dropped my shoulders, and let my heavy hair press against the headrest. The steady drone of diesel combustion and of tires on asphalt played a lullaby in my ears and I fell, once again, sound asleep.

Acknowledgements

Special thanks to:

Thomas Hampson, Christa Ludwig, James Levine, and Gustavo Dudamel – whose interpretations of Mahler provide the soundtrack to this script.

Henry-Louis de la Grange, for every word of his that I have read online since beginning this project. I sincerely hope that many of my readers will buy his books to compensate him financially for the spiritual wealth that I have taken from him *gratis*.

Professor Don Sparling, for his kindness to me in 1990 and for more of the same in 2008. Don volunteered to let his razor-sharp eye fall on this manuscript prior to publication, and graciously agreed to avert that eye whenever I requested that he do so. Any errors that remain in this text are my own, and cannot be blamed on its editor.

My beautiful wife, who did her best to get back to sleep when I got out of bed to work, and who never asked to see what I had to show for my restless efforts and her many lonely hours. And who must perhaps fight her own demons as she reads about the demons of my past, and the darkness that I lived in before I met her. I wish, for her sake and mine, that I could have left a few of these chapters out. But that would have left this story incomplete and insincere. It is a story that many men need to hear. Whether they are of the camp that tries to bury their sins or the one that boasts about them, they need to know that neither works. They need to face up to the truth, and to know that they are not alone. And that God really *can* forgive them. Hopefully their wives can too.

My children, who must soon understand their father and his past far better than they'd prefer.

The infinite *I AM,* Who has showered His blessings on the Czechs, on my nation, and on me. May He continue to do so, despite our forgetful ingratitude and our abject unworthiness.

Suggested Reading, Watching, & Listening

Books

    Milan Kundera: *The Joke, The Book of Laughter and Forgetting*

    Václav Havel: *The Art of the Impossible*

    Thomas Merton: *The Seven Storey Mountain*

    St. Augustine: *Confessions*

Films

    Ladislav Grosman: *The Shop on Main Street*

    Jiři Menzel: *Closely Watched Trains*

    Miloš Forman: *The Firemen's Ball*

    Jana Ševčíková: *Old Believers*

Music

    Bedřich Smetana: *Má vlast, The Bartered Bride*

    Gustav Mahler: *Symphony #2, Symphony #3, Rückert Lieder.* If you dare, *Das Lied von der Erde.* Please be careful with that one.

POSTSCRIPT

(A public speech delivered on August 28, 1999)

This is the time when I am supposed to give thanks. Well, I've got an awful lot to be thankful for, so sit back and relax – this may take a while.

First, to all of you for being here. Thank you for sharing this special day with me and with Deb.

And, of course, my parents. They have done so much to make this occasion special for us, and hosted a rehearsal dinner last night that moved me so much it made me wonder if I'd be able to speak to you today. I'm still not sure.

But that is just the latest thing I have to thank them for. The greatest, of course, is life. But so much more than physical life, they have shaped my inner life: with 33 years of patient love, including five and a half years of wandering and expensive education. If I have any eloquence at all today, it is thanks to them. Most of all, Mom and Dad, thank you for all the things I never thanked you for. There are many.

Next, to all the people who have helped us pull this day off. Special thanks to Carla, Werner, Jurg, and Natalie. They've been with us, at this spot, from the beginning of our engagement; and have graciously offered this beautiful reception hall. As well as months of intensive preparation.

And to Reverend Tim Avery, who has done an incredible job

preparing Deb and I for our wedding; but more importantly, for our marriage.

And this brings me to God. That we are here today is His miracle, and we should all give thanks to Him for making this day happen. A miracle. That I am here is a miracle. For 33 years God has patiently taught me, and spoke to me – even when I was not listening. Through His son Jesus Christ He has forgiven me. And through it all He was preparing me for this, the happiest day of my life.

Last, but first in *my* heart, I'd like to thank my wife. Thank you Deborah. Thank you for saying yes.